The Verge: A Play In Three Acts...

Susan Glaspell

Nabu Public Domain Reprints:

THE VERGE

THE VERGE

A PLAY IN THREE ACTS

BY

SUSAN GLASPELL

BOSTON
SMALL, MAYNARD & COMPANY
PUBLISHERS

Printed in the United States of America

THE MURRAY PRINTING COMPANY
CAMBRIDGE, MASS.

THE VERGE

A PLAY IN THREE ACTS

BY

SUSAN GLASPELL

PERSONS OF THE PLAY

Anthony
Harry Archer (*Claire's husband*)
Hattie (*The Maid*)
Claire
Dick (*Richard Demming*)
Tom Edgeworthy
Elizabeth (*Claire's Daughter*)
Adelaide (*Claire's Sister*)
Dr. Emmons

THE VERGE

ACT ONE

The Curtain lifts on a place that is dark, save for a shaft of light from below which comes up through an open trap door in the floor. This slants up and strikes the long leaves and the huge brilliant blossom of a strange plant whose twisted stem projects from right front. Nothing is seen except this plant and its shadow. A violent wind is heard. A moment later a buzzer. It buzzes once long and three short. Silence. Again the buzzer. Then from below — his shadow blocking the light, comes ANTHONY, *a rugged man past middle life; — he emerges from the stairway into the darkness of the room. Is dimly seen taking up a phone.*

ANTHONY

Yes, Miss Claire? — I'll see.

> [*He brings a thermometer to the stairway for light, looks sharply, then returns to the phone.*

It's down to forty-nine. The plants are in danger —

> [*With great relief and approval.*

Oh, that's fine!

> [*Hangs up the receiver.*

Fine!

> [*He goes back down the stairway, closing the trap-door upon himself, and the curtain is drawn upon darkness and wind.*

[*It opens a moment later on the greenhouse in the sunshine of a snowy morning. The snow piled outside is at times blown through the air. The frost has made patterns on the glass as if — as Plato would have it — the patterns inherent in abstract nature and behind all life had to come out, not only in the creative heat within, but in the creative cold on the other side of the glass. And the wind makes patterns of sound around the glass house.*

The back wall is low; the glass roof slopes sharply up. There is an outside door, a little toward the right. From outside two steps lead down to it. At left a glass partition and a door into the inner room. One sees a little way into this room. At right there is no dividing wall save large plants and vines, a narrow aisle between shelves of plants leads off.

This is not a greenhouse where plants are being displayed, nor the usual workshop for the growing of them, but a place for experiment with plants, a laboratory.

At the back grows a strange vine. It is arresting rather than beautiful. It creeps along the low wall, and one branch gets a little way up the glass. You might see the form of a cross in it, if you happened to think it that way. The leaves of this vine are not the form that leaves have been. They are at once repellent and significant.

ANTHONY is at work preparing soil — mixing, sifting. As the wind tries the door he goes anxiously to the thermometer, nods as if reassured and returns to his work. The buzzer sounds. He starts to answer the telephone, remembers something, halts and listens sharply. It does not buzz once long and three short. Then he returns to his work. The buzzer goes on and on in impatient jerks which mount in anger. Several times ANTHONY is almost compelled by this insistence, but the thing that holds him back is stronger. At last, after a particularly mad splutter, to which ANTHONY longs to make retort, the buzzer gives it up. ANTHONY goes on preparing soil.

A moment later the glass door swings violently in, snow blowing in, and also MR. HARRY ARCHER, wrapped in a rug.

ANTHONY

Oh, please close the door, sir.

HARRY

Do you think I'm not trying to?

[*He holds it open to say this.*]

ANTHONY

But please *do*. This stormy air is not good for the plants.

HARRY

I suppose it's just the thing for me! Now, what do you mean, Anthony, by not answering the phone when I buzz for you?

ANTHONY

Miss Claire — Mrs. Archer told me not to.

HARRY

Told you not to answer me?

ANTHONY

Not you especially — nobody but her.

HARRY

Well I like her nerve — and yours.

ANTHONY

You see, she thought it took my mind from my work to be interrupted when I'm out here. And so it does. So she buzzes once long and — Well, she buzzes her way, and all other buzzing —

HARRY

May buzz.

ANTHONY

[*Nodding gravely.*] She thought it would be better for the flowers.

HARRY

I am not a flower — true, but I too need a little attention — and a little heat. Will you please tell me why the house is frigid?

ANTHONY

Miss Claire ordered all the heat turned out here. [*Patiently explaining it to Miss Claire's speechless husband.*] You see the roses need a great deal of heat.

HARRY

[*Reading the thermometer.*] The roses have seventy-three. I have forty-five.

ANTHONY

Yes, the roses need seventy-three.

HARRY

Anthony, this is an outrage!

ANTHONY

I think it is myself; when you consider what we paid for that heating plant — but as long as it is defective — Why, Miss Claire would never have done what she has if she hadn't looked out for her plants in just such ways as this. Have you forgotten that Breath of Life is about to flower?

HARRY

And where's my breakfast about to flower — that's what I want to know.

ANTHONY

Why Miss Claire got up at five o'clock to order the heat turned off from the house.

HARRY

I see you admire her vigilance.

ANTHONY

Oh, I do. [*Fervently.*] I do. Harm was near, and that woke her up.

HARRY

And what about the harm to — [*Tapping his chest.*] Do roses get pneumonia?

ANTHONY

Oh, yes — yes indeed they do. Why, Mr. Archer, look at Miss Claire herself. Hasn't she given her heat to the roses?

HARRY

[*Pulling the rug around him, preparing for the blizzard.*] She has the fire within.

ANTHONY

[*Delighted.*] Now isn't that true! How well you said it. [*With a glare for this appreciation,* HARRY *opens the door. It blows away from him.*] Please do close the door!

HARRY

[*Furiously.*] You think it is the aim of my life to hold it open?

ANTHONY

[*Getting hold of it.*] Growing things need an even temperature.

> [*While saying this he gets the man out into the snow.*
>
> [ANTHONY *consults the thermometer, not as pleased this time as he was before. He then looks minutely at two of the plants — one is a rose, the other a flower without a name because it has not long enough been a flower. Peers into the hearts of them. Then from a drawer under a shelf, takes two paper*

*bags, puts one over each of these
flowers, closing them down at the
bottom. Again the door blows wildly
in, also* HATTIE, *a maid with a
basket.*

ANTHONY

What do you mean — blowing in here like this! Mrs.
Archer has ordered —

HATTIE

Mr. Archer has ordered breakfast served here.
[*She uncovers the basket and takes out an
electric toaster.*

ANTHONY

Breakfast — here? *Eat* — here? Where plants grow?

HATTIE

The plants won't poison him, will they?
[*At a loss to know what to do with things,
she puts the toaster under the strange
vine at the back, whose leaves lift up
against the glass which has frost
leaves on the outer side.*

ANTHONY

[*Snatching it away.*] You — you think you can *cook
eggs* under the Edge Vine?

HATTIE

I guess Mr. Archer's eggs are as important as a vine.
I guess my work's as important as yours.

ANTHONY

There's a million people like you — and like Mr.
Archer. In all the world there is only one Edge Vine.

HATTIE

Well, maybe one's enough. It don't look like nothin' anyhow.

ANTHONY

And you've not got the wit to know that that's why it's the Edge Vine.

HATTIE

You want to look out, Anthony. You talk nutty. Everybody says so.

ANTHONY

Miss Claire don't say so.

HATTIE

No, because she's —

ANTHONY

You talk too much!
[*Door opens, admitting* HARRY, *with a thermos bottle.*

ANTHONY

Please close —
[HARRY *halts his attempt at closing the door to give* ANTHONY *a look.* ANTHONY *gets the door shut.* HARRY, *after looking around for the best place to eat breakfast, moves a box of earth from the table.*

HARRY

Just give me a hand, will you, Hattie?
[*They bring it to the open space and he and* HATTIE *arrange breakfast things,* HATTIE *with triumphant glances at the distressed* ANTHONY.

ANTHONY

[*Deciding he must act.*]   Mr. Archer, this is not the place to eat breakfast!

HARRY

Dead wrong, old boy.   The place that has heat is the place to eat breakfast.   [*To* HATTIE.]   Tell the other gentlemen — I heard Mr. Demming up, and Mr. Edgeworthy, if he appears, that as long as it is such a pleasant morning, we're having breakfast outside. To the conservatory for coffee.   [HATTIE *giggles, is leaving.*]   And let's see, have we got everything? [*Takes the one shaker, shakes a little pepper on his hand. Looks in vain for the other shaker.*]   And tell Mr. Demming to bring the salt.

ANTHONY

Mr. Archer, I am sorry to say anything —

HARRY

[*Who is taking off a bulb and attaching the toaster.*] Then why do you?

ANTHONY

But Miss Claire will be very angry.

HARRY

I am very angry.   Did I choose to eat my breakfast at the other end of a blizzard?

ANTHONY

[*An exclamation of horror at the thermometer.*]   The temperature is falling.   I must report.   [*He punches the buzzer, takes up the phone.*]   Miss Claire?   It is Anthony. A terrible thing has happened.   Mr. Archer — what? Yes, a terrible thing — Yes, it is about Mr. Archer— No — no, not dead.   But here.   He is here.   Yes, he is well, he seems well, but he is eating his breakfast.   Yes,

he is having breakfast served out here — for himself,
and the other gentlemen are to come too — Well, he
seemed to be annoyed because the heat had been
turned off from the house. But the door keeps opening
— this stormy wind blowing right over the plants.
The temperature has already fallen — Yes, yes. I
thought you would want to come.

> [ANTHONY *opens the trap door and goes
> below.* HARRY *looks disapprovingly
> down into this openness at his feet,
> returns to his breakfast.* ANTHONY
> *comes up, bearing a box.*

HARRY

[*Turning his face away.*] Phew! What a smell.

ANTHONY

Yes. Fertilizer has to smell.

HARRY

Well it doesn't have to smell up my breakfast!

ANTHONY

[*With a patient sense of order.*] The smell belongs
here. [*He and the smell go to the inner room.*]

> [*The outer door opens just enough to admit*
> CLAIRE — *is quickly closed. With*
> CLAIRE *in a room another kind of
> aliveness is there.*

CLAIRE

What are you doing here?

HARRY

Getting breakfast.

> [*All the while doing so.*

CLAIRE

I'll not have you in my place!

HARRY

If you take all the heat then you have to take me.

CLAIRE

I'll show you how I have to take you.
[*With her hands begins scooping upon him the soil* ANTHONY *has prepared.*

HARRY

[*Jumping up, laughing, pinning down her arms, putting his arms around her.*] Claire — be decent. What harm do I do here?

CLAIRE

You pull down the temperature.

HARRY

Not after I'm in.

CLAIRE

And you told Tom and Dick to come and make it uneven.

HARRY

Tom and Dick are our guests. We can't eat where it's warm and leave them to eat where it's cold.

CLAIRE

I don't see why not.

HARRY

You only see what you want to see.

CLAIRE

That's not true. I wish it were. No; no, I don't either. [*She is disturbed — that troubled thing which rises from within, from deep, and takes* CLAIRE. *She turns to the Edge Vine, examines. Regretfully to* ANTHONY, *who has come in with a plant.*] It's turning back, isn't it?

ANTHONY

Can you be sure yet, Miss Claire?

CLAIRE

Oh yes — it's had its chance. It doesn't want to be — what hasn't been.

HARRY

[*Who has turned at this note in her voice. Speaks kindly.*] Don't take it so seriously, Claire.

[*Claire laughs.*

CLAIRE

No, I suppose not. But it *does* matter — and why should I pretend it doesn't, just because I've failed with it?

HARRY

Well, I don't want to see it get you — it's not important enough for that.

CLAIRE

[*In her brooding way.*] Anything is important enough for that — if it's important at all. [*To the vine.*] I thought you were out, but you're — going back home.

ANTHONY

But you're doing it this time, Miss Claire. When Breath of Life opens — and we see its heart —

> CLAIRE *looks toward the inner room. Because of intervening plants they do not see what is seen from the front — a plant like caught motion, and of a greater transparency than plants have had. Its leaves, like waves that curl, close around a heart that is not seen.*

*This plant stands by itself in what,
because of the arrangement of things
about it, is a hidden place. But
nothing is between it and the light.*

CLAIRE

Yes, if the heart has [*a little laugh*] held its own, then
Breath of Life is alive in its otherness. But Edge Vine
is running back to what it broke out of.

HARRY

Come have some coffee, Claire.
[ANTHONY *returns to the inner room, the
outer door opens,* DICK *is hurled in.*

CLAIRE

[*Going to the door, as he gasps for breath before closing
it.*] How dare you make my temperature uneven!
[*She shuts the door and leans against it.*]

DICK

Is that what I do?
[*A laugh, a look between them, which is
held into significance.*

HARRY

[*Who is not facing them.*] Where's the salt?

DICK

Oh, I fell down in the snow. I must have left the
salt where I fell. I'll go back and look for it.

CLAIRE

And change the temperature? We don't need salt.

HARRY

You don't need salt, Claire. But we eat eggs.

CLAIRE

I must tell you I don't like the idea of any food being eaten here, where things have their own way to go. Please eat as little as possible, and as quickly.

HARRY

A hostess calculated to put one at one's ease.

CLAIRE

[*With no ill-nature.*] I care nothing about your ease. Or about Dick's ease.

DICK

And no doubt that's what makes you so fascinating a hostess.

CLAIRE

Was I a fascinating hostess last night, Dick? [*Softly sings.*] " Oh, night of love — "
[*From the Barcarole of Tales of Hoffman.*

HARRY

We've got to have salt.
[*He starts for the door.* CLAIRE *slips in ahead of him, locks it, takes the key. He marches off right.*

CLAIRE

[*Calling after him.*] That end's always locked.

DICK

Claire darling, I wish you wouldn't say those startling things. You do get away with it, but I confess it gives me a shock — and really, it's unwise.

CLAIRE

Haven't you learned that the best place to hide is in the truth? [*As* HARRY *returns.*] Why won't you

believe me, Harry, when I tell you the truth — about
doors being locked?

HARRY

Claire, it's selfish of you to keep us from eating salt
just because you don't eat salt.

CLAIRE

[*With one of her swift changes.*] Oh, Harry! Try
your egg without salt. Please — Please try it without
salt!

[*An intensity which seems all out of pro-
portion to the subject.*

HARRY

An egg demands salt.

CLAIRE

" An egg demands salt." Do you know, Harry, why
you are such an unseasoned person? " An egg demands
salt."

HARRY

Well, it doesn't always get it.

CLAIRE

But your spirit gets no lift from the salt withheld.'

HARRY

Not an inch of lift.

[*Going back to his breakfast.*

CLAIRE

And pleased — so pleased with itself, for getting no
lift. Sure it is just the right kind of spirit — because
it gets no lift. [*More brightly.*] But, Dick, you must
have tried your egg without salt.

DICK

I'll try it now.

[*He goes to the breakfast table.*

CLAIRE

You must have tried and tried things. Isn't that the way one leaves the normal, and gets into the byways of perversion.

HARRY

Claire.

DICK

[*Pushing back his egg.*] If so, I prefer to wait for the salt.

HARRY

Claire, there is a *limit*.

CLAIRE

Precisely what I had in mind. To perversion too there is a limit. So — the fortifications are unassailable. If one ever does get out, I suppose it is — quite unexpectedly, and perhaps — a bit terribly.

HARRY

Get out where?

CLAIRE

[*With a bright smile.*] Where you, darling, will never go.

HARRY

And from which you, darling, had better beat it.

CLAIRE

I wish I could. [*To herself.*] No — no I don't either.

> [*Again this troubled thing turns her to the plants. She puts by themselves the two which* ANTHONY *covered with paper bags. Is about to remove these papers.* HARRY *strikes a match.*

CLAIRE

[*Turning sharply.*] You can't smoke here. The plants are not used to it.

HARRY

Then I should think smoking would be just the thing for them.

CLAIRE.

There is design.

HARRY

[*To Dick.*] Am I supposed to be answered? I never can be quite sure at what moment I am answered.

> [*They both watch* CLAIRE, *who has uncovered the plants and is looking intently into the flowers. From a drawer she takes some tools. Very carefully gives the rose pollen to an unfamiliar flower — rather wistfully unfamiliar, which stands above on a small shelf near the door of the inner room.*]

DICK

What is this you're doing, Claire?

CLAIRE

Pollenizing. Crossing for fragrance.

DICK

It's all rather mysterious, isn't it?

HARRY

And Claire doesn't make it any less so.

CLAIRE

Can I make life any less mysterious?

HARRY

If you know what you are doing, why can't you tell Dick?

DICK

Never mind. After all, why should I be told?

[*He turns away.*
[*At that she wants to tell him. Helpless, as one who cannot get across a stream, starts uncertainly.*

CLAIRE

I want to give fragrance to Breath of Life — [*Faces the room beyond the wall of glass.*] — the flower I've created that is outside what flowers have been. What has gone out should bring fragrance from what it has left. But no definite fragrance, no limiting enclosing thing. I call the fragrance I am trying to create — Reminiscence. [*Her hand on the pot of the wistful little flower she has just given pollen.*] Reminiscent of the rose, the violet, arbutus — but a new thing — itself. Breath of Life may be lonely out in what hasn't been. Perhaps some day I can give it reminiscence.

DICK

I see, Claire.

CLAIRE

I wonder if you do.

HARRY

Now, Claire, you're going to be gay today, aren't you? These are Tom's last couple of days with us.

CLAIRE

That doesn't make me especially gay.

HARRY

Well, you want him to remember you as yourself, don't you?

CLAIRE

I would like him to. Oh — I would like him to!

HARRY

Then be amusing. That's really you, isn't it Dick?

DICK

Not quite all of her — I should say.

CLAIRE

[*Gayly.*] Careful, Dick. Aren't you indiscreet?
Harry will be suspecting that I am your latest strumpet.

HARRY

Claire! What language you use! A person knowing you only by certain moments could never be made
to believe you are a refined woman.

CLAIRE

True, isn't it, Dick?

HARRY

It would be a good deal of a lark to let them listen
in at times — then tell them that here is the flower of
New England!

CLAIRE

Well, if this is the flower of New England, then the
half has never been told.

DICK

About New England?

CLAIRE

I thought I meant that. Perhaps I meant — about
me.

HARRY

[*Going on with his own entertainment.*] Explain that
this is what came of the men who made the laws that

made New England, that here is the flower of those
gentlemen of culture who —

DICK

Moulded the American mind!

CLAIRE

Oh!

[It is pain.

HARRY

Now what's the matter?

CLAIRE

I want to get away from them!

HARRY

Rest easy, little one — you do.

CLAIRE

I'm not so sure — that I do. But it *can* be done!
We need not be held in forms molded for us. There is
outness — and otherness.

HARRY

Now, Claire — I didn't mean to start anything
serious.

CLAIRE

No; you never mean to do that. I want to break it
up! I tell you, I want to break it up! If it were all in
pieces, we'd be [*A little laugh*] shocked to aliveness —
[*To Dick*] wouldn't we? There would be strange new
comings together — mad new comings together, and
we would know what it is to be born, and then we
might know — that we are. Smash it. [*Her hand is
near an egg.*] As you'd smash an egg.

> [*She pushes the egg over the edge of the
> table and leans over and looks, as over
> a precipice.*

HARRY

[*With a sigh.*]   Well, all you've smashed is the egg, and all that amounts to is that now Tom gets no egg. So that's that.

CLAIRE

[*With difficulty, drawing herself back from the fascination of the precipice.*]   You think I can't smash anything?   You think life can't break up, and go outside what it was?   Because you've gone dead in the form in which you found yourself, you think that's all there is to the whole adventure?   And that is called sanity. And made a virtue — to lock one in.   You never worked with things that grow!   Things that take a sporting chance — go mad — that sanity mayn't lock them in — from life untouched — from life — that waits. [*She turns toward the inner room.*]   Breath of Life.

[*She goes in there.*

HARRY

Oh, I wish Claire wouldn't be strange like that. [*Helplessly.*]   What is it?   What's the matter?

DICK

It's merely the excess of a particularly rich temperament.

HARRY

But it's growing on her.   I sometimes wonder if all this — [*Indicating the place around him.*]   is a good thing.   It would be all right if she'd just do what she did in the beginning — make the flowers as good as possible of their kind.   That's an awfully nice thing for a woman to do — raise flowers.   But there's something about this — changing things into other things — putting things together and making queer new things — this —

DICK

Creating?

HARRY

Give it any name you want it to have— it's unsettling for a woman. They say Claire's a shark at it, but what's the good of it, if it gets her? What *is* the good of it, anyway? Suppose we can produce new things. Lord — look at the old ones we've got. [*Looks outside; turns back.*] Heavens, what a noise the wind does make around this place. [*But now it is not all the wind, but* TOM EDGEWORTHY, *who is trying to let himself in at the locked door, their backs are to him.*] I want my egg. You can't eat an egg without salt. I must say I don't get Claire lately. I'd like to have Charlie Emmons see her — he's fixed up a lot of people. shot to pieces in the war. Claire needs something to tone her nerves *up*. You think it would irritate her?

DICK

She'd probably get no little entertainment out of it.

HARRY

Yes, dog-gone her, she would. [TOM *now takes more heroic measures to make himself heard at the door.*] Funny — how the wind can fool you. Now by not looking around I could imagine — why I could imagine anything. Funny, isn't it, about imagination? And Claire says I haven't got any!

DICK

It would make an amusing drawing — what the wind makes you think is there. [*First makes forms with his hands, then leveling the soil prepared by* ANTHONY, *traces lines with his finger.*] Yes, really — quite jolly.
[TOM, *after a moment of peering in at them, smiles, goes away.*

HARRY

You're another one of the queer ducks, aren't you?

Come now — give me the dirt. Have you queer ones really got anything — or do you just put it over on us that you have? [DICK *smiles, draws on.*] Not saying anything, eh? Well, I guess you're wise there. If you keep mum — how we going to prove there's nothing there?

DICK

I don't keep mum. I draw.

HARRY

Lines that don't make anything — how can they tell you anything? Well, all I ask is, don't make Claire queer. Claire's a first water good sport — really, so don't encourage her to be queer.

DICK

Trouble is, if you're queer enough to be amusing, it might — open the door to queerness.

HARRY

Now don't say things like that to Claire.

DICK

I don't have to.

HARRY

Then *you* think she's queer, do you? Queer as you are, you think she's queer. I would like to have Dr. Emmons come out. [*After a moment of silently watching* DICK, *who is having a good time with his drawing.*] You know, frankly, I doubt if you're a good influence for Claire. [DICK *lifts his head ever so slightly.*] Oh, I don't worry a bit about — things a husband might worry about. I suppose an intellectual woman — and for all Claire's hate on her ancestors, she's got the bug herself. Why she has times of boring into things until she doesn't know you're there. What do you think I caught her doing the other day? Reading Latin. Well

— a woman that reads Latin needn't worry a husband much.

DICK

They said a good deal in Latin.

HARRY·

But I was saying, I suppose a woman who lives a good deal in her mind never does have much — well, what you might call passion.. [*Uses the word as if it shouldn't be used. Brows knitted, is looking ahead, does not see* DICK's *face. Turning to him with a laugh.*] I suppose you know pretty much all there is to know about women?

DICK

Perhaps one or two details have escaped me.

HARRY

Well, for that matter, you might know all there is to know about women and not know much about Claire. But now about — [*does not want to say passion again*] — oh, feeling — Claire has a certain — well, a certain —

DICK

Irony?

HARRY

Which is really more— more —

DICK

More fetching, perhaps.

HARRY

Yes! Than the thing itself. But of course — you wouldn't have much of a thing that you have irony about.

DICK

Oh — wouldn't you! I mean — a man might.

HARRY

I'd like to talk to Edgeworthy about Claire. But it's not easy to talk to Tom about Claire — or to Claire about Tom.

DICK

[*Alert.*]   They're very old friends, aren't they?

HARRY

Why — yes, they are. Though they've not been together much of late years, Edgeworthy always going to the ends of the earth to — meditate about something. I must say I don't get it. If you have a place — that's the place for you to be. And he did have a place — best kind of family connections, and it was a very good business his father left him. Publishing business — in good shape, too, when old Edgeworthy died. I wouldn't call Tom a great success in life — but Claire does listen to what he says.

DICK

Yes, I've noticed that.

HARRY

So, I'd like to get him to tell her to quit this queer business of making things grow that never grew before.

DICK

But are you sure that's what he would tell her. Isn't he in the same business himself?

HARRY

Why he doesn't raise anything.
                         [TOM *is again at the door.*

DICK

Anyway I think he might have some idea that we can't very well reach each other.

HARRY

Damn nonsense. What have we got intelligence for?

DICK

To let each other alone, I suppose. Only we haven't enough to do it.

> [TOM *is now knocking on the door with a revolver.* HARRY *half turns, decides to be too intelligent to turn.*]

HARRY

Don't tell me I'm getting nerves. But the way some of you people talk is enough to make even an aviator jumpy. Can't reach each other! Then we're fools. If I'm here and you're there why can't we reach each other?

DICK

Because I am I and you are you.

HARRY

No wonder your drawing's queer. A man who can't reach another man —

> [TOM *here reaches them by pointing the revolver in the air and firing it.* DICK *digs his hand into the dirt.* HARRY *jumps to one side, fearfully looks around.* TOM, *with a pleased smile to see he at last has their attention, moves the handle to indicate he would be glad to come in.*]

HARRY

Why — it's Tom! What the — ? [*Going to the door.*] He's locked out. And Claire's got the key. [*Goes to the inner door, tries it.*] And she's locked in! [*Trying to see her in there.*] Claire! Claire! [*Returning to the outer door.*] Claire's got the key — and I can't get to Claire. [*Makes a futile attempt at getting the door open without a key, goes back to inner door — peers, pounds.*] Claire! Are you there? Didn't you hear the revolver? Has she gone down cellar? [*Tries the trap door.*] Bolted! Well I love the way she keeps people locked out!

DICK

And in.

HARRY

[*Getting angry, shouting at the trap door.*] Didn't you hear the revolver? [*Going to* TOM.] Awfully sorry, old man, but — [*In astonishment to* DICK.] He can't hear me. [TOM, *knocking with the revolver to get their attention makes a gesture of inquiry with it.*] No — no — no! Is he asking if he shall shoot himself? [*Shaking his head violently.*] Oh, no — no! Um — *um!*

DICK

Hardly seems a man would shoot himself because he can't get to his breakfast.

HARRY

I'm coming to believe people would do anything! [TOM *is making another inquiry with the revolver.*] *No!* not here. Don't shoot yourself. [*Trying hard to get the word through.*] *Shoot* yourself. I mean — don't. [*Petulantly to* DICK.] It's ridiculous that you can't make a man understand you when he looks right at you like that. [*Turning back to* TOM.] Read my lips. Lips. I'm saying — Oh damn. Where is Claire? All right — I'll explain it with motions. We wanted the salt. . . . [*Going over it to himself.*] and Claire wouldn't let us go out for it on account of the temperature. Salt. Temperature. [*Takes his egg-cup to the door, violent motion of shaking in salt.*] But — no — [*Shakes his head.*] No salt. [*He then takes the thermometer, a flower pot, holds them up to* TOM.] On account of the temperature. Tem-per-a —[TOM *is not getting it*.] Oh — well, what can you do when a man don't *get* a thing? [TOM *seems to be preparing the revolver for action*. HARRY *pounds on the inner door*.] Claire! Do you want Tom to shoot himself?

[*As he looks in there, the trap door lifts, and* CLAIRE *comes half-way up*.]

CLAIRE

Why, what is Tom doing out there, with a revolver?

HARRY

He is about to shoot himself because you've locked him out from his breakfast.

CLAIRE

He must know more interesting ways of destroying himself. [*Bowing to* TOM.] Good morning. [*From his side of the glass* TOM *bows and smiles back*.] Isn't it strange — our being in here — and he being out there?

HARRY

Claire, have you no ideas of hospitality? Let him in!

CLAIRE

In? Perhaps that isn't hospitality.

HARRY

Well, whatever hospitality is, what is out there is snow — and wind — and our guest — who was asked to come here for his breakfast. To think a man has to *say* such things.

CLAIRE

I'm going to let him in. Though I like his looks out there.

[*She takes the key from her pocket.*

HARRY

Thank heaven the door's coming open. Somebody can go for salt, and we can have our eggs.

CLAIRE

And open the door again — to let the salt in? No. If you insist on salt tell Tom now to go back and get it. It's a stormy morning and there'll be just one opening of the door.

HARRY

How can we tell him what we can't make him hear? And why does he think we're holding this conversation instead of letting him in?

CLAIRE

It would be interesting to know. I wonder if he'll tell us?

HARRY

Claire! Is this any time to wonder anything?

CLAIRE

Give up the idea of salt for your egg and I'll let him in.

> [Holds up the key to TOM to indicate that
> for her part she is quite ready to let
> him in.]

HARRY

I want my egg!

CLAIRE

Then ask him to bring the salt. It's quite simple.

> [HARRY goes through another pantomime
> with the egg cup and the missing
> shaker. CLAIRE, still standing half
> way down cellar, sneezes. HARRY
> growing all the while less amiable,

explains with thermometer and flower pot that there can only be one opening of the door. TOM *looks interested, but unenlightened. But suddenly he smiles, nods, vanishes.*

HARRY

Well, thank heaven [*Exhausted*] that's over.

CLAIRE

[*Sitting on the top step.*] It was all so queer. He locked out on his side of the door. You locked in on yours. Looking right at each other and —

HARRY

[*In mockery.*] And me trying to tell him to kindly fetch the salt!

CLAIRE

Yes.

HARRY

[*To* DICK.] Well, I didn't do so bad a job, did I? Quite an idea, explaining our situation with the thermometer and the flower pot. That was really an apology for keeping him out there. Heaven knows — some explanation was in order. [*He is watching and sees* TOM *coming.*] Now there he is, Claire. And probably pretty well fed up on weather.

> [CLAIRE *goes to the door, stops before it. She and* TOM *look at each other through the glass. Then she lets him in.*

TOM

And now I am in. For a time it seemed I was not to be in. But after I got the idea, that you were keeping me out there to see if I could get the idea — it would be too humiliating for a wall of glass to keep one from understanding.   [*Taking it from his pocket.*]   So there's the other thermometer.   Where do you want it?

                             [CLAIRE *takes it.*

CLAIRE

And where's the pepper?

TOM

[*Putting it on the table.*]   And here's the pepper.

HARRY

Pepper?

TOM

When Claire sneezed I knew —

CLAIRE

Yes, I knew if I sneezed you would bring the pepper.

TOM

Funny, how one always remembers the salt, but the pepper gets overlooked in preparations.   And what is an egg without pepper?

HARRY

[*Nastily.*]   There's your egg, Edgeworthy.   [*Pointing to it on the floor.*]   Claire decided it would be a good idea to smash everything, so she began with your egg.

TOM

[*Looking at his egg.*]   The idea of smashing everything is really more intriguing than an egg.

HARRY

Nice that you feel that way about it.

CLAIRE

[*Giving* TOM *his coffee.*]   You want to hear something amusing?   I married Harry because I thought he would smash something.

HARRY

Well, that was an error in judgment.

CLAIRE

I'm such a naive trusting person — [HARRY *laughs* — CLAIRE *gives him a surprised look, continues simply.*] Such a guileless soul that I thought flying would do something to a man. But it didn't take us out. We just took it in.

TOM

It's only our own spirit can take us out.

HARRY

Whatever you mean by out.

CLAIRE

[*After looking intently at* TOM, *and considering it.*] But our own spirit is not something on the loose. Mine isn't. It has something to do with what I do. To fly. To be free in air. To look from above on the world of all my days. Be where man has never been! Yes — wouldn't you think the spirit could get the idea? The earth grows smaller. I am leaving. What are they — running around down there? Why do they run around down there? Houses? Houses are funny lines and down-going slants — houses are vanishing slants. I am alone. Can I breathe this rarer air? Shall I go higher? Shall I go too high? I am loose. I am out. But no; man flew, and returned to earth the man who left it.

HARRY

And jolly well likely not to have returned at all if he'd had those flighty notions while operating a machine.

CLAIRE

Oh, Harry! [*Not lightly asked.*] Can't you see it would be better not to have returned than to return the man who left it?

HARRY

I have some regard for human life.

CLAIRE

Why no — I am the one who has the regard for human life. [*More lightly.*] That was why I swiftly divorced my stick-in-the-mud artist and married — the man of flight. But I merely passed from a stick-in-the-mud artist to a —

DICK

Stick-in-the-air aviator?

HARRY

Speaking of your stick-in-the-mud artist, as you romantically call your first blunder, isn't his daughter — and yours — due here today?

CLAIRE

I knew something was disturbing me. Elizabeth. A daughter is being delivered unto me this morning. I have a feeling it will be more painful than the original delivery. She has been, as they quaintly say, educated; prepared for her place in life.

HARRY

And fortunately Claire has a sister who is willing to give her young niece that place.

CLAIRE

The idea of giving anyone a place in life.

HARRY

Yes! The very idea!

CLAIRE

Yes! [*As often, the mocking thing gives true expression to what lies somberly in her.*] The war. There was another gorgeous chance.

HARRY

Chance for what? I call you, Claire. I ask you to say what you mean.

CLAIRE

I don't know — precisely. If I did — there'd be no use saying it.

[*At* HARRY's *impatient exclamation she turns to* TOM.]

TOM

[*Nodding.*] The only thing left worth saying is the thing we can't say.

HARRY

Help!

CLAIRE

Yes. But the war didn't help. Oh, it was a stunning chance! But fast as we could — scuttled right back to the trim little thing we'd been shocked out of.

HARRY

You bet we did — showing our good sense.

CLAIRE

Showing our incapacity — for madness.

HARRY

Oh, come now Claire — snap out of it. You're not really trying to say that capacity for madness is a good thing to *have?*

CLAIRE

[*In simple surprise.*] Why yes, of course.

DICK

But I should say the war did leave enough madness to give you a gleam of hope.

CLAIRE

Not the madness that — breaks through. And it was — a stunning chance! Mankind massed to kill. We have failed. We are through. We will destroy. Break this up — it can't go farther. In the air above — in the sea below — it is to kill! All we had thought we were — we aren't. We were shut in with what wasn't so. Is there one ounce of energy has not gone to this killing? Is there one love not torn in two? Throw it in! Now? Ready? Break up. Push. Harder. Break up. And then — and then —! But we didn't say — "And then — " The spirit didn't take the tip.

HARRY

Claire! Come now — [*Looking to the others for help.*] Let's talk of something else.

CLAIRE

Plants do it. The big leap — it's called. Explode their species — because something in them knows they've gone as far as they can go. Something in them knows they're shut in to just that. So — go mad — that life may not be prisoned. Break themselves up — into crazy things — into lesser things, and from the pieces — may come one sliver of life with vitality to find the future. How beautiful. How brave.

TOM

[*As if he would call her from too far — or would let her know he has gone with her.*] Claire!

CLAIRE

[*Her eyes turning to him.*] Why should we mind lying under the earth? We who have no such initiative —

no proud madness? Why think it death to lie under life so flexible — so ruthless and ever-renewing?

ANTHONY

[*From the door of the inner room.*] Miss Claire?

CLAIRE

[*After an instant.*] Yes?
> [*She goes with him, as they disappear his voice heard, " show me now . . . want those violets bedded."*]

HARRY

Oh, this has got to *stop*. I've got to — put a stop to it some way. Why Claire used to be the best sport a man ever played around with. I can't stand it to see her getting hysterical.

TOM

That was not hysterical.

HARRY

What was it then — I want to know?

TOM

It was — a look.

HARRY

Oh, I might have known I'd get no help from either of you. Even you, Edgeworthy — much as she thinks of you — and fine sort as I've no doubt you are, you're doing Claire no good — encouraging her in these queer ways.

TOM

I couldn't change Claire if I would.

HARRY

And wouldn't if you could.

TOM

No. But you don't have to worry about me. I'm
going away in a day or two. And I shall not be back.

HARRY

Trouble with you is, it makes a little difference
whether you're here or away. Just the fact of your
existence does encourage Claire in this — this way
she's going.

TOM

[*With a smile.*] But you wouldn't ask me to go so
far as to stop my existence? Though I would do that
for Claire — if it were the way to help her.

HARRY

By Jove, you say that as if you meant it.

TOM

Do you think I would say anything about Claire.
I didn't mean?

HARRY

You think a lot of her, don't you? [TOM *nods.*
You don't mean — [*A laugh letting him say it.*] that
you're — in love with Claire?

TOM

In love? Oh, that's much too easy. Certainly I do
love Claire.

HARRY

Well, you're a cool one!

TOM

Let her be herself. Can't you see she's troubled?

HARRY

Well, what is there to trouble Claire? Now I ask
you. It seems to me she has everything.

TOM

She's left so — open. Too exposed. [*As* HARRY *moves impatiently*.] Please don't be annoyed with me. I'm doing my best at saying it. You see Claire isn't hardened into one of those forms she talks about. She's too — aware. Always pulled toward what could be — tormented by the lost adventure.

HARRY

Well, there's danger in all that. Of course there's danger, Tom. But you can't help that.

HARRY

Claire was the best fun a woman could be. Is yet — at times.

TOM

Let her be — at times. As much as she can and will. She does need that. Don't keep her from it by making her feel you're holding her in it. Above all, don't try to stop what she's doing here. If she can do it with plants, perhaps she won't have to do it with herself.

HARRY

Do what?

TOM

[*Low, after a pause*.] Break up what exists. Open the door to destruction in the hope of — a door on the far side of destruction.

HARRY

Well, you give me the willies. [*Moves around in irritation, troubled. To* ANTHONY, *who is passing through with a sprayer*.] Anthony, have any arrangements been made about Miss Claire's daughter?

ANTHONY

I haven't heard of any arrangements.

HARRY

Well, she'll have to have some heat in her room. We can't all live out here.

ANTHONY

Indeed you can not. It is not good for the plants.

HARRY

I'm going where I can *smoke*.

[*Goes out.*

DICK

[*Lightly, but fascinated by the idea.*] You think there is a door on the — hinter side of destruction?

TOM

How can one tell — where a door may be. One thing I want to say to you — for it is about you. [*Regards* DICK *and not with his usual impersonal contemplation.*] I don't think Claire should have — any door closed to her. [*Pause.*] You know, I think, what I mean. And perhaps you can guess how it hurts to say it. Whether it's — mere escape within, — rather shameful escape within, or the wild hope of that door through, it's — [*Suddenly all human.*] Be good to her! [*After a difficult moment, smiles.*] Going away forever is like dying, so one can say things.

DICK

Why do you do it — go away forever?

TOM

I haven't succeeded here.

DICK

But you've tried the going away before.

TOM

Never knowing I would not come back. So that wasn't going away. My hope is that this will be like looking at life from outside life.

DICK

But then you'll not be in it.

TOM

I haven't been able to look at it while in it.

DICK

Isn't it more important to be in it than to look at it?

TOM

Not what I mean by look.

DICK

It's hard for me to conceive of — loving Claire and going away from her forever.

TOM

Perhaps it's harder to do than to conceive of.

DICK

Then why do it?

TOM

It's my only way of keeping her.

DICK

I'm afraid I'm like Harry now. I don't get you.

TOM

I suppose not. Your way is different. [*With calm, with sadness — not with malice.*] But I shall have her longer. And from deeper.

DICK

I know that.

TOM

Though I miss much. Much. [*The buzzer.* TOM *looks around to see if anyone is coming to answer it, then goes to the phone.*] Yes? . . . I'll see if I can get to her. [*To* DICK.] Claire's daughter has arrived. [*Looking in the inner room — returns to phone.*] I don't see her. [*Catching a glimpse of* ANTHONY *off right.*] Oh, Anthony, where's Miss Claire? Her daughter has arrived.

ANTHONY

She's working at something very important in her experiments.

DICK

But isn't her daughter one of her experiments?

ANTHONY

[*After a baffled moment.*] Her daughter is finished.

TOM

[*At the phone.*] Sorry — but I can't get to Claire. She appears to have gone below. [ANTHONY *closes the trap door.*] I did speak to Anthony, but he says that Claire is working at one of her experiments and that her daughter is finished. I don't know how to make her hear. — I took the revolver back to the house. Anyway you will remember Claire doesn't answer the revolver. I hate to reach Claire when she doesn't want to be reached. Why of course — a daughter is very important, but oh, that's too bad. [*Putting down the receiver.*] He says the girl's feelings are hurt. Isn't that annoying? [*Gingerly pounds on the trap door. Then with the other hand. Waits,* ANTHONY *has a gentle smile for the gentle tapping — nods approval as* TOM *returns to the phone.*] She doesn't come up. Indeed I did — with both fists — Sorry.

ANTHONY

Please, you won't try again to disturb Miss Claire, will you?

DICK

Her daughter is here, Anthony. She hasn't seen her daughter for a year.

ANTHONY

Well, if she got along without a mother for a year —
[*Goes back to his work.*

DICK

[*Smiling after* ANTHONY.] Plants are queer. Perhaps it's safer to do it with pencil — [*Regards* TOM.] Or with pure thought. Things that grow in the earth —

TOM

[*Nodding.*] I suppose because we grew in the earth.

DICK

I'm always shocked to find myself in agreement with Harry, but I too am worried about Claire — and this.
[*Looking at the plants.*

TOM

It's her best chance.

DICK

Don't you hate to go away to India — forever — leaving Claire's future uncertain?

TOM

You're cruel now. And you knew that you were being cruel.

DICK

Yes, I like the lines of your face when you suffer.

TOM

The lines of yours when you're causing suffering — I don't like them.

DICK

Perhaps that's your limitation.

TOM

I grant you it may be. [*They are silent.*] I had an odd feeling then that you and I sat here once before, long ago, and that we were plants. And you were a beautiful plant, and I — I was a very ugly plant. I confess it surprised me — finding myself so ugly a plant.

> [*A young girl is seen outside.* HARRY *gets the door open for her and brings* ELIZABETH *in.*

HARRY

There's heat here. And two of your mother's friends. Mr. Demming — Richard Demming — the artist — and I think you and Mr. Edgeworthy are old friends.

> [ELIZABETH *comes forward. She is the creditable young American — well built, poised, " cultivated," so sound an expression of the usual as to be able to meet the world with assurance — assurance which training has made rather graceful. She is about seventeen — and mature. You feel solid things behind her.*

TOM

I knew you when you were a baby. You used to kick a great deal then.

ELIZABETH

[*Laughing, with ease.*]   And scream, I haven't a doubt. But I've stopped that. One does, doesn't one? And it was you who gave me the idol.

TOM

Proselyting, I'm afraid.

ELIZABETH

I beg — ? Oh — *yes.* [*Laughing cordially.*] I *see.*
[*she doesn't.*] I dressed the idol up in my dolls' clothes.
They fitted perfectly — the idol was just the size of my
doll Ailine. But mother didn't like the idol that way,
and tore the clothes getting them off. [*To* HARRY,
after looking around.] Is mother here?

HARRY

[*Crossly.*] Yes, she's here. Of course she's here.
And she must know you're here.
[*After looking in the inner room he goes to
the trap door and makes a great noise.*

ELIZABETH

Oh — *please.* Really — it doesn't make the least
difference.

HARRY

Well, all I can say is, your manners are better than
your mother's.

ELIZABETH

But you see I don't do anything interesting, so I have
to have good manners. [*Lightly, but leaving the impres-
sion there is a certain superiority in not doing anything
interesting. Turning cordially to* DICK.] My father
was an artist.

DICK

Yes, I know.

ELIZABETH

He was a portrait painter. Do you do portraits?

DICK

Well, not the kind people buy.

ELIZABETH

They bought father's.

DICK

Yes, I know he did that kind.

HARRY

[*Still irritated.*]   Why, you don't do portraits.

DICK

I did one of you the other day.   You thought it was a milk-can.

ELIZABETH

[*Laughing delightedly.*]   No?   Not really?   Did you think — How *could* you think — [*As* HARRY *does not join the laugh.*]   Oh, I beg your pardon.   I — Does mother grow beautiful roses now?

HARRY

No, she does not.
>   [*The trap door begins to move.* CLAIRE'S
>   head appears.*]

ELIZABETH

Mother!   It's been so long —
>   [*She tries to overcome the difficulties and
>   embrace her mother.*

CLAIRE

[*Protecting a box she has.*]   Careful, Elizabeth.   We mustn't upset the lice.

ELIZABETH

[*Retreating.*]   *Lice?*   [*But quickly equal even to lice.*] Oh — *yes.*   You take it — them — off plants, don't you?

CLAIRE

I'm putting them on certain plants.

ELIZABETH

[*Weakly.*]   Oh, I thought you took them off.

CLAIRE

[*Calling.*]   Anthony!   [*He comes.*]   The lice.
> [*He takes them from her.*
> [CLAIRE, *who has not fully ascended, looks
> at* ELIZABETH, *hesitates, then suddenly
> starts back down the stairs.*

HARRY

[*Outraged.*]   Claire!   [*Slowly she re-ascends — sits on
> the top step.*]   [*After a long pause in
> which he has waited for* CLAIRE *to
> open a conversation with her daughter.*]
Well, and what have you been doing at school all this
time?

ELIZABETH

Oh — studying.

CLAIRE

Studying what?

ELIZABETH

Why — the things one studies, mother.

CLAIRE

Oh! The things one studies.
> [*Looks down cellar again.*

DICK

[*After another wait.*]   And what have you been doing
besides studying?

ELIZABETH

Oh — the things one does. Tennis and skating and
dancing and —

CLAIRE

The things one does.

ELIZABETH

Yes. All the things. The — the things one does.
Though I haven't been in school these last few months,
you know. Miss Lane took us to Europe.

TOM

And how did you like Europe?

ELIZABETH

[*Capably.*] Oh, I thought it was awfully amusing.
All the girls were quite mad about Europe. Of course,
I'm glad I'm an American.

CLAIRE

Why?

ELIZABETH

[*Laughing.*] Why — mother! Of course one is glad
one is an American. All the girls —

CLAIRE

[*Turning away.*] O—h!

[*A moan under the breath.*

ELIZABETH

Why, mother — aren't you well?

HARRY

Your mother has been working pretty hard at all
this.

ELIZABETH

Oh, I do so want to know all about it? Perhaps I can
help you! I think it's just awfully amusing that you're
doing something. One does now-a-days, doesn't one?
— if you know what I mean. It was the war, wasn't it,
made it the thing to do something.

DICK

[*Slyly*.] And you thought, Claire, that the war was lost.

ELIZABETH

The *war? Lost!* [*Her capable laugh*.] Fancy our losing a war! Miss Lane says we should give *thanks*. She says we should each do some expressive thing —you know what I mean? And that this is the *keynote* of the age. Of course, one's own kind of thing. Like mother — growing flowers.

CLAIRE

You think that is one's own kind of thing?

ELIZABETH

Why of course I do, mother. And so does Miss Lane. All the girls —

CLAIRE

[*Shaking her head as if to get something out*.] S—hoo.

ELIZABETH

What is it, mother?

CLAIRE

A fly shut up in my ear — " All the girls!"

ELIZABETH

[*Laughing*.] Mother was always so amusing. So *different* — if you know what I mean. Vacations I've lived mostly with Aunt Adelaide, you know.

CLAIRE

My sister who is fitted to rear children.

HARRY

Well, somebody has to do it.

ELIZABETH

And I do love Aunt Adelaide, but I think it's going to be awfully amusing to be around with mother now — and help her with her work. Help do some useful beautiful thing.

CLAIRE

I am not doing any useful beautiful thing.

ELIZABETH

Oh, but you are, mother. Of course you are. Miss Lane says so. She says it is your splendid heritage gives you this impulse to do a beautiful thing for the race. She says you are doing in your way what the great teachers and preachers behind you did in theirs.

CLAIRE

[*Who is good for little more.*]   Well all I can say is, Miss Lane is stung.

ELIZABETH

Mother! What a thing to say of Miss *Lane*. [*From this slipping into more of a little girl manner.*]   Oh, she gave me a speil one day about living up to the men I come from.

[CLAIRE *turns and regards her daughter.*

CLAIRE

You'll do it, Elizabeth.

ELIZABETH

Well, I don't know. Quite a job, I'll say. Of course, I'd have to do it in my way. I'm not going to teach or preach or be a stuffy person. But now that — [*She here becomes the product of a superior school.*] values have shifted and such sensitive new things have been liberated in the world —

CLAIRE

[*Low.*]   Don't use those words.

ELIZABETH

Why — why not?

CLAIRE

Because you don't know what they mean.

ELIZABETH

Why of course I know what they mean!

CLAIRE

[*Turning away.*]   You're — stepping on the plants.

HARRY

[*Hastily.*]   Your mother has been working awfully hard at all this.

ELIZABETH

Well, now that I'm here you'll let me help you, won't you, mother?

CLAIRE

[*Trying for control.*]   You needn't — bother.

ELIZABETH

But I *want* to. Help add to the wealth of the world.

CLAIRE

Will you please get it out of your head that I am adding to the wealth of the world!

ELIZABETH

But, mother — of course you are. To produce a new and better kind of plants —

CLAIRE

They may be new. I don't give a damn whether they're better.

ELIZABETH

But — but what are they then?

CLAIRE

[*As if choked out of her.*] They're different.

ELIZABETH

[*Thinks a minute, then laughs triumphantly.*] But what's the use of making them different if they aren't better?

HARRY

A good square question, Claire. Why don't you answer it?

CLAIRE

I don't have to answer it.

HARRY

Why not give the girl a fair show? You never have, you know. Since she's interested, why not tell her what it is you're doing?

CLAIRE

She is not interested.

ELIZABETH

But I am, mother. Indeed I am. I do want awfully to understand what you are doing, and help you.

CLAIRE

You can't help me, Elizabeth.

HARRY

Why not let her try?

CLAIRE

Why do you ask me to do that? This is my own thing. Why do you make me feel I should — [*Goes to* ELIZABETH.] I will be good to you, Elizabeth. We'll go around together. I haven't done it, but — you'll see. We'll do gay things. I'll have a lot of beaus around for you. Anything else. Not — this is — Not this.

ELIZABETH

As you like, mother, of course. I just would have been so glad to — to share the thing that interests you.
[*Hurt borne with good-breeding and a smile.*

HARRY

Claire!

[*Which says, " How can you? "*

CLAIRE

[*Who is looking at* ELIZABETH.]   Yes, I will try.

TOM

I don't think so. As Claire says— anything else.

ELIZABETH

Why of course — I don't at all want to intrude.

HARRY

It'll do Claire good to take someone in. To get down to brass tacks and actually say what she's driving at.

CLAIRE

Oh — *Harry*. But yes — I will try. [*Does try, but no words come. Laughs.*] When you come to say it it's not — One would rather not nail it to a cross of words —[*Laughs again.*] with brass tacks.

HARRY

[*Affectionately.*] But I want to see you put things into words, Claire, and realize just where you are.

CLAIRE

[*Oddly.*] You think that's a — good idea?

ELIZABETH

[*In her manner of holding the world capably in her hands.*] Now let's talk of something else. I hadn't the least idea of making mother feel badly.

CLAIRE

[*Desperately.*] No, we'll go on. Though I don't know — where we'll end. I can't answer for that. These plants — [*Beginning flounderingly.*] perhaps they are less beautiful — less sound — than the plants from which they diverged. But they have found — otherness. [*Laughs a little shrilly.*] If you know — what I mean.

TOM

Claire — stop this! [*To* HARRY.] This is wrong.

CLAIRE

[*Excitedly.*] No; I'm going on. They have been shocked out of what they were — into something they were not; they've broken from the forms in which they found themselves. They are alien. Outside. That's it, outside; if you — know what I mean?

ELIZABETH

[*Not shocked from what she is.*] But of course, the object of it all is to make them better plants. Otherwise, what would be the sense in doing it?

CLAIRE

[*Not reached by* ELIZABETH.] Out there — [*Giving it with her hands.*] lies all that's not been touched — lies life that waits. Back here — the old pattern, done again, again and again. So long done it doesn't even know itself for a pattern — in immensity. But this — has invaded. Crept a little way into — what wasn't. Strange lines in life unused. And when you make a pattern new you know a pattern's made with life. And then you know that anything may be — if only you know how to reach it.

> [*This has taken form, not easily, but with great struggle between feeling and words.*]

HARRY

[*Cordially.*] Now I begin to get you, Claire. I never knew before why you called it the Edge Vine.

CLAIRE

I should destroy the Edge Vine. It isn't — over the edge. It's running back to — " all the girls." It's a little afraid of Miss Lane. [*Looking somberly at it.*] You are out, but you are not alive.

ELIZABETH

Why it looks all right, mother.

CLAIRE

Didn't carry life with it from the life it left. Dick — you know what I mean. At least you ought to. [*Her ruthless way of not letting anyone's feelings stand in the way of truth.*] Then destroy it for me! It's hard to do it — with the hands that made it.

DICK

But what's the point in destroying it, Claire?

CLAIRE

[*Impatiently.*] I've told you. It cannot create.

DICK

But you say you can go on producing it, and it's interesting in form.

CLAIRE

And you think I'll stop with that? Be shut in — with different life — that can't creep on? [*After trying to put destroying hands upon it.*] It's hard to — get past what we've done. Our own dead things — block the way.

TOM

But you're doing it this next time, Claire. [*Nodding to the inner room.*] In there!

CLAIRE

[*Turning to that room.*] I'm not sure.

TOM

But you told me Breath of Life has already reproduced itself. Doesn't that show it has brought life from the life it left?

CLAIRE

But timidly, rather — wistfully. A little homesick. If it is less sure this time, then it is going back to — Miss Lane. But if the pattern's clearer now, then it has made friends life that waits. I'll know tomorrow.

ELIZABETH

You know, something tells me this is *wrong*.

CLAIRE

The hymn-singing ancestors are tuning up.

ELIZABETH

I don't know what you mean by that mother, but —

CLAIRE

But we will now sing, " Nearer my God to Thee; Nearer to — "

ELIZABETH

[*Laughingly breaking in.*] Well, I don't care. Of course you can make fun of me, but something does tell me this is wrong. To do what — what —

DICK

What God did?

ELIZABETH

Well — yes. Unless you do it to make them better — to do it just to *do* it — that doesn't seem right to me.

CLAIRE

[*Roughly.*] "Right to you!" And that's all you know of adventure — and of anguish. Do you know it is you — world of which you're so true a flower — makes me have to leave? You're there to hold the door shut! Because you're young and of a gayer world, you think I can't *see* them — those old men? Do you know why you're so sure of yourself? Because you can't *feel*. Can't feel — the limitless — out there — a sea just over the hill. I will not stay with you! [*Buries her hands in the earth around the Edge Vine. But suddenly steps back from it as she had from* ELIZABETH.] And I will not stay with *you!*

> [*Grasps it as we grasp what we would kill, is trying to pull it up. They all step forward in horror.* ANTHONY *is drawn in by this harm to the plant.*

ANTHONY

Miss Claire! Miss Claire! The work of years!

CLAIRE

May only make a prison! [*Struggling with* HARRY, *who is trying to stop her.*] You think I too will die on the edge? [*She has thrown him away, is now struggling with the vine.*] Why did I make you? To get past you!

[*As she twists it.*] Oh yes, I know you have thorns! The Edge Vine should have thorns.

> [*With a long tremendous pull for deep roots, she has it up. As she holds the torn roots.*]

Oh, I have loved you so! You took me where I hadn't been.

ELIZABETH

[*Who has been looking on with a certain practical horror.*] Well, I'd say it would be better not to go there!

CLAIRE

Now I know what you are for!

> [*Flings her arm back to strike* ELIZABETH *with the Edge Vine.*]

HARRY

[*Wresting it from her.*] Claire! Are you *mad?*

CLAIRE

No, I'm not mad. I'm — too sane! [*Pointing to* ELIZABETH — *and the words come from mighty roots.*] To think that object ever moved my belly and sucked my breast!

> [ELIZABETH *hides her face as if struck.*

HARRY

[*Going to* ELIZABETH, *turning to* CLAIRE.] This is atrocious! You're cruel.

> [*He leads* ELIZABETH *to the door and out. After an irresolute moment in which he looks from* CLAIRE *to* TOM, DICK *follows.* ANTHONY *cannot bear to go. He stoops to take the Edge Vine from the floor.* CLAIRE's *gesture stops him. He goes into the inner room.*

CLAIRE

[*Kicking the Edge Vine out of her way, drawing deep breath, smiling.*] O—h. How good I feel! Light! [*A movement as if she could fly.*] Read me something, Tom dear. Or say something pleasant — about God. But be very careful what you say about him! I have a feeling — he's not far off.

[CURTAIN]

ACT TWO

Late afternoon of the following day. CLAIRE is alone in the tower — a tower which is thought to be round but does not complete the circle. The back is curved, then jagged lines break from that, and the front is a queer bulging window — in a curve that leans. The whole structure is as if given a twist by some terrific force — like something wrung. It is lighted by an old-fashioned watchman's lantern hanging from the ceiling; the innumerable pricks and slits in the metal throw a marvelous pattern on the curved wall — like some masonry that hasn't been.

There are no windows at back, and there is no door save an opening in the floor. The delicately distorted rail of a spiral staircase winds up from below. CLAIRE is seen through the huge ominous window as if shut into the tower. She is lying on a seat at the back looking at a book of drawings. To do this she has left the door of her lantern a little open — and her own face is drawing clearly seen.

A door is heard opening below; laughing voices, CLAIRE listens, not pleased.

ADELAIDE

[*Voice coming up.*] Dear — dear, why do they make such twisting steps.

HARRY

Take your time, most up now. [HARRY's *head appears, he looks back.*] Making it all right?

ADELAIDE

I can't tell yet — [*Laughingly.*] No, I don't think so.

HARRY

[*Reaching back a hand for her.*]   The last lap — is
the bad lap.

[ADELAIDE *is up, and occupied with getting
her breath.*

HARRY

Since you wouldn't come down, Claire, we thought
we'd come up.

ADELAIDE

[*As* CLAIRE *does not greet her.*]   I'm sorry to intrude,
but I have to see you, Claire.   There are things to be —
arranged.   [CLAIRE *volunteering nothing about arrangements*, ADELAIDE *surveys the tower.   An unsympathetic
eye goes from the curves to the lines which diverge.   Then
she looks from the window.*]   Well, at least you have a
view.

HARRY

This the first time you've been up here?

ADELAIDE

Yes, in the five years you've had the house I was
never asked up here before.

CLAIRE

[*Amiably enough.*]   You weren't asked up here now.

ADELAIDE

Harry asked me.

CLAIRE

It isn't Harry's tower.   But never mind — since you
don't like it — it's all right.

ADELAIDE

[*Her eyes again rebuking the irregularities of the
tower.*]   No, I confess I do not care for it.   A round
tower should go on being round

HARRY

Claire calls this the thwarted tower. She bought the house because of it. [*Going over and sitting by her, his hand on her ankle.*] Didn't you, old girl? She says she'd like to have known the architect.

ADELAIDE

Probably a tiresome person too incompetent to make a perfect tower.

CLAIRE

Well, now he's disposed of, what next?

ADELAIDE

[*Sitting down in a manner of capably opening a conference.*] Next, Elizabeth, and you, Claire. Just what is the matter with Elizabeth?

CLAIRE

[*Whose voice is cool, even, as if herself is not really engaged by this.*] Nothing is the matter with her. She is a tower that is a tower.

ADELAIDE

Well, is that anything against her?

CLAIRE

She's just like one of her father's portraits. They never interested me. Nor does she.
            [*Looks at the drawings which do interest her.*

ADELAIDE

A mother cannot cast off her own child simply because she does not interest her!

CLAIRE

[*An instant raising cool eyes to* ADELAIDE.] Why can't she?

ADELAIDE

Because it would be monstrous!

CLAIRE

And why can't she be monstrous — if she has to be?

ADELAIDE

You don't have to be. That's where I'm out of patience with you, Claire. You are really a particularly intelligent, competent person, and it's time for you to call a halt to this nonsense and be the woman you were meant to be!

CLAIRE

[*Holding the book up to see another way.*] What inside dope have you on what I was meant to be?

ADELAIDE

I know what you came from.

CLAIRE

Well, isn't it about time somebody got loose from that? What I came from made you, so —

ADELAIDE

[*Stiffly.*] I see.

CLAIRE

So — you being such a tower of strength, why need I too be imprisoned in what I came from?

ADELAIDE

It isn't being imprisoned. Right there is where you make your mistake, Claire. Who's in a tower — in an unsuccessful tower? Not I. I go about in the world — free, busy, happy. Among people. I have no time to think of myself.

CLAIRE

No.

ADELAIDE

No. My family. The things that interest them; from morning till night it's——

CLAIRE

Yes, I know you have a large family, Adelaide; five, and Elizabeth makes six.

ADELAIDE

We'll speak of Elizabeth later. But if you would just get out of yourself and enter into other people's lives —

CLAIRE

Then I would become just like you. And we should all be just alike in order to assure one another that we're all just right. But since you and Harry and Elizabeth and ten million other people bolster each other up, why do you especially need me?

ADELAIDE

[*Not unkindly.*] We don't need you as much as you need us.

CLAIRE

[*A wry face.*]   I never liked what I needed.

HARRY

I am convinced I am the worst thing in the world for you, Claire.

CLAIRE

[*With a smile for his tactics, but shaking her head.*] I'm afraid you're not. I don't know — perhaps you are.

ADELAIDE

Well, what is it you want, Claire?

CLAIRE

[*Simply.*]   You wouldn't know if I told you.

ADELAIDE

That's rather arrogant.

HARRY

Yes, take a chance, Claire. I have been known to get an idea — and Adelaide quite frequently gets one.

CLAIRE

[*The first resentment she has shown.*] You two feel very superior, don't you?

ADELAIDE

I don't think we are the ones who are feeling superior.

CLAIRE

Oh, yes, you are. Very superior to what you think is my feeling of superiority, comparing my — isolation with your " heart of humanity." Soon we will speak of the beauty of common experiences, of the — Oh, I could say it all before we come to it.

HARRY

Adelaide came up here to help you, Claire.

CLAIRE

Adelaide came up here to lock me in. Well, she can't do it.

ADELAIDE

[*Gently.*] But can't you see that one may do that to one's self?

CLAIRE

[*Thinks of this, looks suddenly tired — then smiles.*] Well, at least I've changed the keys.

HARRY

" Locked in." Bunkum. Get that out of your head. Claire. Who's locked in? Nobody that I know of, We're all free Americans. Free as air.

ADELAIDE

I wish you'd come and hear one of Dr. Morley's sermons, Claire. You're very old-fashioned if you think sermons are what they used to be.

CLAIRE

[*With interest.*] And do they still sing " Nearer my God to Thee?"

ADELAIDE

They do, and a noble old hymn it is. It would do you no harm at all to sing it.

CLAIRE

[*Eagerly.*] Sing it to me, Adelaide. I'd like to hear you sing it.

ADELAIDE

It would be sacrilege to sing it to you in this mood.

CLAIRE

[*Falling back.*] Oh, I don't know. I'm not so sure God would agree with you. That would be one on you, wouldn't it?

ADELAIDE

It's easy to feel one's self set apart!

CLAIRE

No, it isn't.

ADELAIDE

[*Beginning anew.*] It's a new age, Claire. Spiritual values —

CLAIRE

Spiritual values! [*In her brooding way.*] So you have pulled that up. [*With cunning.*] Don't think I don't know what it is you do.

ADELAIDE

Well, what do I do? I'm sure I have no idea what you're talking about.

HARRY

[*Affectionately, as* CLAIRE *is looking with intentness at what he does not see.*] What does she do, Claire?

CLAIRE

It's rather clever, what she does. Snatching the phrase — [*A movement as if pulling something up.*] standing it up between her and — the life that's there. And by saying it enough. — " We have life! We have life! We have life! " Very good come-back at one who would really be — " Just so! *We* are that. Right this way, please —" That, I suppose, is what we mean by needing each other. All join in the chorus, " This is it! This is it! This is it! " And anyone who won't join is to be — visited by relatives. [*Regarding* ADELAIDE *with curiosity.*] Do you really think that anything is going on in you?

ADELAIDE

[*Stiffly.*] I am not one to hold myself up as a perfect example of what the human race may be.

CLAIRE

[*Brightly.*] Well, that's good.

HARRY

Claire!

CLAIRE

Humility's a *real* thing — not just a fine name for laziness.

HARRY

Well Lord A'mighty, you can't call Adelaide lazy.

CLAIRE

She stays in one place because she hasn't the energy
to go anywhere else.

ADELAIDE

[*As if the last word in absurdity has been said.*]   *I*
haven't energy?

CLAIRE

[*Mildly.*]   You haven't any energy at all, Adelaide.
That's why you keep so busy.

ADELAIDE

Well — Claire's nerves are in a worse state than I had
realized.

CLAIRE

So perhaps we'd better look at Blake's drawings.
[*Takes up the book.*

ADELAIDE

It would be all right for me to look at Blake's drawings.   You'd better look at the Sistine Madonna.
[*Affectionately, after she has watched* CLAIRE'S *face a
moment.*]   What is it, Claire?   Why do you shut yourself out from us?

CLAIRE

I told you.   Because I do not want to be shut in with
you.

ADELAIDE

All of this is not very pleasant for Harry.

HARRY

I want Claire to be *gay*.

CLAIRE

Funny — you should want that.   [*Speaks unwillingly,
a curious, wistful unwillingness.*]   Did you ever say a
preposterous thing, then go trailing after the thing
you've said and find it wasn't so preposterous?   Here

is the circle we are in. [*Describes a big circle.*] Being
gay. It shoots little darts through the circle, and a
minute later — gayety all gone, and you looking
through that little hole the gayety left.

ADELAIDE

[*Going to her, as she is still looking through that little
hole.*] Claire, dear, I wish I could make you feel how
much I care for you. [*Simply, with real feeling.*] You
can call me all the names you like — dull, common-
place, lazy — that *is* a new idea, I confess, but the rest
of our family's gone now, and the love that used to be
there between us all — the only place for it now is
between you and me. You were so much loved, Claire.
You oughtn't to try and get away from a world in
which you are so much loved. [*To* HARRY.] Mother,
— Father — all of us, always loved Claire best. We
always loved Claire's queer gayety. Now you've got
to hand it to us for that, as the children say.

CLAIRE

[*Moved, but eyes shining with a queer bright loneliness.*]
But never one of you — once — looked with me through
the little pricks the gayety made — never one of you
— once, looked with me at the queer light that came
in through the pricks.

ADELAIDE

And can't you see, dear, that it's better for us we
didn't? And that it would be better for you now if you
would just resolutely look somewhere else? You must
see yourself that you haven't the poise of people who
are held — well, within the circle, if you choose to put
it that way. There's something about being in that
main body, having one's roots in the big common experiences, gives a calm which you have missed. That's
why I want you to take Elizabeth, forget yourself, and

CLAIRE

I do want calm. But mine would have to be a calm
I — worked my way to. A calm all prepared for me —
would stink.

ADELAIDE

[*Less sympathetically.*] I know you have to be yourself, Claire. But I don't admit you have a right to hurt
other people.

HARRY

I think Claire and I had better take a nice long trip.

ADELAIDE

Now why don't you?

CLAIRE

I am taking a trip.

ADELAIDE

Well, Harry isn't, and he'd like to go and wants you
to go with him. Go to Paris and get yourself some
awfully good-looking clothes — and have one grand
fling at the gay world. You really love that, Claire,
and you've been awfully dull lately. I think that's the
whole trouble.

HARRY

I think so too.

ADELAIDE

This sober business of growing plants —

CLAIRE

Not sober — it's mad.

ADELAIDE

All the more reason for quitting it.

CLAIRE

But madness that is the only chance for sanity.

ADELAIDE

Come, come, now — lets not juggle words.

CLAIRE

[*Springing up.*] How dare you say that to me, Adelaide. You who are such a liar and thief and whore with words!

ADELAIDE

[*Facing her, furious.*] How *dare* you —

HARRY

Of course not, Claire. You have the most preposterous way of using words.

CLAIRE

I respect words.

ADELAIDE

Well, you'll please respect me enough not to dare use certain words to me!

CLAIRE

Yes, I do dare. I'm tired of what you do — you and all of you. Life — experience — values — calm — sensitive words which raise their heads as indications. And you *pull them up* — to decorate your stagnant little minds — and think that makes you — And because you have pulled that word from the life that grew it you won't let one who's honest, and aware, and troubled, try to reach through to — to what she doesn't know is there. [*She is moved, excited, as if a cruel thing has been done.*] Why did you come up here?

ADELAIDE

To try and help you. But I begin to fear I can't do it. It's pretty egotistical to claim that what so many people are, is wrong.

[CLAIRE, *after looking intently at* ADE-
LAIDE, *slowly, smiling a little, describes a circle. With deftly used
hands makes a quick, vicious break
in the circle which is there in the air.*

HARRY

[*Going to her, taking her hands.*] It's getting close
to dinner time. You were thinking of something else,
Claire, when I told you Charlie Emmons was coming
to dinner tonight. [*Answering her look.*] Sure — he is
a neurologist, and I want him to see you. I'm perfectly
honest with you — cards all on the table, you know
that. I'm hoping if you like him — and he's the best
scout in the world, that he can help you. [*Talking
hurriedly against the stillness which follows her look from
him to* ADELAIDE, *where she sees between them an " understanding " about her.*] Sure you need help, Claire.
Your nerves are a little on the blink — from all you've
been doing. No use making a mystery of it — or a
tragedy. Emmons is a cracker-jack, and naturally
I want you to get a move on yourself and be happy
again.

CLAIRE

[*Who has gone over to the window.*] And this neurologist can make me happy?

HARRY

Can make you well — and then you'll be happy.

ADELAIDE

[*In the voice of now fixing it all up.*] And I just had
an idea about Elizabeth. Instead of working with mere
plants, why not think of Elizabeth as a plant and —
[CLAIRE, *who has been looking out the
window now throws open one of the
panes that swings out — or seems to
and calls down in great excitement.*

CLAIRE

Tom! *Tom!* Quick! Up here! I'm in trouble!

HARRY

[*Going to the window.*] That's a rotten thing to do, Claire! You've frightened him.

CLAIRE

Yes, how fast he can run. He was deep in thought and I stabbed right through.

HARRY

Well, he'll be none too pleased when he gets up here and finds there was no reason for the stabbing!
[*They wait for his footsteps, HARRY annoyed, ADELAIDE offended, but stealing worried looks at CLAIRE, who is looking fixedly at the place in the floor where TOM will appear. — Running footsteps.*]

TOM

[*His voice getting there before he does.*] Yes, Claire — yes — yes — [*As his head appears.*] What is it?

CLAIRE

[*At once presenting him and answering his question.*] My sister.

TOM

[*Gasping.*] Oh, — why — is that all? I mean —how do you do? Pardon, I [*Panting.*] came up — rather hurriedly.

HARRY

If you want to slap Claire, Tom, I for one have no objection.

CLAIRE

Adelaide has the most interesting idea, Tom. She proposes that I take Elizabeth and roll her in the gutter. Just let her lie there until she breaks up into —

ADELAIDE

Claire! I don't see how — even in fun — pretty vulgar fun — you can speak in those terms of a pure young girl. I'm beginning to think I had better take Elizabeth.

CLAIRE

Oh, I've thought that all along.

ADELAIDE

And I'm also beginning to suspect that — oddity may be just a way of shifting responsibility.

CLAIRE

[*Cordially interested in this possibility.*] Now you know — that might be.

ADELAIDE

A mother who does not love her own child! You are an unnatural woman, Claire.

CLAIRE

Well, at least it saves me from being a natural one.

ADELAIDE

Oh — I know, you think you have a great deal! But let me tell you, you've missed a great deal! You've never known the faintest stirring of a mother's love.

CLAIRE

That's not true.

HARRY

No. Claire loved our boy.

CLAIRE

I'm glad he didn't live.

HARRY

[*Low.*] Claire!

CLAIRE

I loved him. Why should I want him to live?

HARRY

Come, dear, I'm sorry I spoke of him — when you're not feeling well.

CLAIRE

I'm feeling all right. Just because I'm seeing something, it doesn't mean I'm sick.

HARRY

Well, let's go down now. About dinner time. I shouldn't wonder if Emmons were here. [*As* ADELAIDE *is starting down stairs.*] Coming, Claire?

CLAIRE

No.

HARRY

But it's time to go down for dinner.

CLAIRE

I'm not hungry.

HARRY

But we have a guest. Two guests — Adelaide's staying, too.

CLAIRE

Then you're not alone.

HARRY

But I invited Dr. Emmons to meet you.

CLAIRE

[*Her smile flashing.*] Tell him I am violent tonight.

HARRY

Dearest — how can you joke about such things!

CLAIRE

So you do think they're serious?

HARRY

[*Irritated.*] No, I do not! But I want you to come down for dinner!

ADELAIDE

Come, come, Claire; you know quite well this is not the sort of thing one does.

CLAIRE

Why go on saying one doesn't, when you are seeing one does? [*To Tom.*] Will you stay with me a while? I want to purify the tower.
[ADELAIDE *begins to disappear.*

HARRY

Fine time to choose for a tête-à-tête. [*As he is leaving.*] I'd think more of you, Edgeworthy, if you refused to humor Claire in her ill-breeding.

ADELAIDE

[*Her severe voice coming from below.*] It is not what she was taught.

CLAIRE

No, it's not what I was taught. [*Laughing rather timidly.*] And perhaps you'd rather have your dinner?

TOM

No.

CLAIRE

We'll get something later. I want to talk to you.
[*But she does not — laughs.*] Absurd that I should feel
bashful with you. Why am I so awkward with words
when I go to talk to you?

TOM

The words know they're not needed.

CLAIRE

No, they're not needed. There's something underneath — an ·open way — down below the way that
words can go.   [*rather desperately.*]   It is there, isn't it?

TOM

Oh, yes, it is there.

CLAIRE

Then why do we never — go it?

TOM

If we went it, it would not be there.

CLAIRE

Is that true? How terrible, if that is true.

TOM

Not terrible, wonderful — that it should — of itself
— be there.

CLAIRE

[*With the simplicity that can say anything.*]   I want
to go it, Tom, I'm lonely up on top here. Is it that I
have more faith than you, or is it only that I'm greedier?
You see you don't know — [*Her reckless laugh.*] what
you're missing. You don't know how I could love you.

TOM

Don't, Claire; that isn't — how it is — between you
and me.

CLAIRE

But why can't it be — every way — between you and me?

TOM

Because we'd lose — the open way. [*The quality of his denial shows how strong his feeling for her.*] With anyone else — not with you.

CLAIRE

But you are the only one I want. The only one — all of me wants.

TOM

I know; but that's the way it is.

CLAIRE

You're cruel.

TOM

Oh, Claire, I'm trying so hard to — save it for us. Isn't it our beauty and our safeguard that underneath our separate lives, no matter where we may be, with what other, there is this open way between us? That's so much more than anything we could bring to being.

CLAIRE

Perhaps. But — it's different with me. I'm not — all spirit.

TOM

[*His hand on her.*] Dear!

CLAIRE

No, don't touch me — since — [*Moving.*] you're going away tomorrow? [*He nods.*] For — always? [*His head just moves assent.*] India is just another country. But there are undiscovered countries.

TOM

Yes, but we are so feeble we have to reach our country through the actual country lying nearest Don't you do that yourself, Claire? Reach your country through the plants' country?

CLAIRE

My country? You mean — Outside?

TOM

No, I don't think it that way.

CLAIRE

Oh, yes, you do.

TOM

Your country is the inside, Claire. The innermost. You are disturbed because you lie too close upon the heart of life.

CLAIRE

[Restlessly.] I don't know; you can think it one way — or another. No way says it, and that's good — at least it's not shut up in saying.
[She is looking at her enclosing hand, as if something is shut up there.

TOM

But also, you know, things may be freed by expression. Come from the unrealized into the fabric of life.

CLAIRE

Yes, but why does the fabric of life have to — freeze into its pattern? It should — [doing it with her hands.] flow [Then turning like an unsatisfied child to him.] But I wanted to talk to you.

TOM

You are talking to me. Tell me about your flower that never was before — your Breath of Life?

CLAIRE

I'll know tomorrow. You'll not go until I know?

TOM

I'll try to stay.

CLAIRE

It seems to me, if it has — then I have, integrity in — [*Smiles, it is as if the smile lets her say it.*]   otherness. I don't want to die on the edge!

TOM

Not you!

CLAIRE

Many do. It's what makes them too smug in all-ness — those dead things on the edge, died, distorted — trying to get through. Oh — don't think I don't see — The Edge Vine! [*A pause, then swiftly.*] Do you know what I mean? Or do you think I'm just a fool, or crazy?

TOM

I think I know what you mean, and you know I don't think you are a fool, or crazy.

CLAIRE

Stabbed to awareness! — no matter where it takes you, isn't that more than a safe place to stay? [*Telling him very simply despite the pattern of pain in her voice.*]· Anguish may be a thread — making patterns that haven't been. A thread — blue and burning.

TOM

[*To take her from what even he fears for her.*] But you were telling me about the flower you breathed to life. What is your Breath of Life?

CLAIRE

[*An instant playing.*] It's a secret. A secret? — it's a trick. Distilled from the most fragile flowers there

are. It's only air — pausing — playing; except, far in,
one stab of red, its quivering heart — that asks a
question. But here's the trick — I bred the air — form
to strength. The strength shut up behind us I've sent
— far out. [*Troubled.*] I'll know tomorrow. And I
have another gift for Breath of Life; some day —
though days of work lie in between — some day I'll
give it reminiscence. Fragrance that is — no one thing
in here but — reminiscent. [*Silence, she raises wet
eyes.*] We need the haunting beauty from the life
we've left. I need that. [*He takes her hands and
breathes her name.*] Let me reach my country with
you. I'm not a plant. After all, they don't — accept
me. Who does — accept me? Will you?

Tom

My dear — dear, dear, Claire — you move me so!
You stand alone in a clearness that breaks my heart.
[*Her hands move up his arms. He takes them to hold
them from where they would go — though he can hardly
do it.*] But you've asked what you yourself could
answer best. We'd only stop in the country where
everyone stops.

Claire

We might come through — to radiance.

Tom

Radiance in an enclosing place.

Claire

Perhaps radiance lighting forms undreamed. [*Her
reckless laugh.*] I'd be willing to — take a chance, I'd
rather lose than never know.

Tom

No, Claire. Knowing you from underneath, I know
you couldn't bear to lose.

CLAIRE

Wouldn't men say you were a fool!

TOM

They would.

CLAIRE

And perhaps you are. [*He smiles a little.*] I feel so desperate, because if only I could — show you what I am, you might see I could have without losing. But I'm a stammering thing with you.

TOM

You do show me what you are.

CLAIRE

I've known a few moments that were life. Why don't they help me now? One was in the air. I was up with Harry — flying — high. It was about four months before David was born — the doctor was furious — pregnant women are supposed to keep to earth. We were going fast — I *was* flying — I had left the earth. And then — within me, movement, for the first time — stirred to life far in air — movement within. The man unborn, he too, would fly. And so — I always loved him. He was movement — and wonder. In his short life were many flights. I never told anyone about the last one. His little bed was by the window — he wasn't four years old. It was night, but him not asleep. He saw the morning star — you know — the morning star. Brighter — stranger — reminiscent — and a promise. He pointed — " Mother," he asked me, " what is there — beyond the stars? " A baby, a sick baby — the morning star. Next night — the finger that pointed was — [*Suddenly bites her own finger.*] But, yes, I am glad. He would always have tried to move and too much would hold him. Wonder would die — and he'd laugh at soaring. [*Looking down, sidewise.*] Though I liked his voice. So I wish you'd stay near me — for I like your voice, too.

TOM
Claire! That's — [*Choked.*] almost too much.

CLAIRE
[*One of her swift changes — canny, almost practical.*] Well, I'm glad if it is. How can I make it more? [*But what she sees brings its own change.*] I know what it is you're afraid of. It's because I have so much — yes, why shouldn't I say it? — passion. You feel that in me, don't you? You think it would swamp everything. But that isn't all there is to me.

TOM
Oh, I know it! My dearest — why it's because I know it! You think I *am* — a fool?

CLAIRE
It's a thing that's — sometimes more than I am. And yet I — I am more than it is.

TOM
I know. I know about you.

CLAIRE
I don't know that you do. Perhaps if you really knew about me — you wouldn't go away.

TOM
You're making me suffer, Claire.

CLAIRE
I know I am. I want to. Why shouldn't you suffer? [*Now seeing it more clearly than she has ever seen it.*] You know what I think about you? You're afraid of suffering, and so you stop this side — in what you persuade yourself is suffering. [*Waits, then sends it*

straight.] You know — how it is — with me and Dick? [*As she sees him suffer.*] Oh, no, I don't want to hurt you! Let it be you! I'll teach you — you needn't scorn it. It's rather wonderful.

Tom
Stop that, Claire! That isn't you.

Claire
Why are you so afraid — of letting me be low — if that is low? You see — [*Cannily.*] I believe in beauty. I have the faith that can be bad as well as good. And you know why I have the faith? Because sometimes — from my lowest moments — beauty has opened as the sea. From a cave I saw immensity.
My love, you're going away —
Let me tell you how it is with me;
I want to touch you — somehow touch you once before I die —
Let me tell you how it is with me.
   I do not want to work,
I want to be;
Do not want to make a rose or make a poem —
Want to lie upon the earth and know.
            [*Closes her eyes.*]
Stop doing that! — words going into patterns;
They do it sometimes when I let come what's there.
Thoughts take pattern — then the pattern is the thing.
But let me tell you how it is with me.
            [*It flows again.*]
All that I do or say — it is to what it comes from, —
A drop lifted from the sea.
I want to lie upon the earth and know.
But — scratch a little dirt and make a flower;
Scratch a bit of brain — something like a poem.
            [*Covering her face.*]
Stop *doing* that.   Help me stop doing that!

TOM

[*And from the place where she had carried him.*
Don't talk at all. Lie still and know —.
And know that I am knowing.

CLAIRE

Yes; but we are so weak we have to talk;
To talk — to touch.
Why can't I rest in knowing I would give my life to
    reach you?
That has — all there is.
But I must — put my timid hands upon you,
Do something about infinity.
Oh, let what will flow into us,
And fill us full — and leave us still.
Wring me dry,
And let me fill again with life more pure.
To know — to feel,
And do nothing with what I feel and know —
That's being good. That's nearer God.
    [*Drenched in the feeling that has flowed through her —
but surprised — helpless.*] Why, I said your thing,
didn't I? Opened my life to bring you to me, and what
came — is what sends you away.

TOM

No! What came is what holds us together. What
came is what saves us from ever going apart. [*Brokenly.*]
My beautiful one. You — you brave flower of all our
knowing.

CLAIRE

I am not a flower. I am too torn. If you have
anything — Help me. Breathe. Breathe the healing
oneness, and let me know in calm.
    [*With a sob his head rests upon her.*

Claire

[*Her hands on his head, but looking far.*] Beauty —
you pure one thing. Breathe — Let me know in calm.
Then — trouble me, trouble me — for other moments
— in father calm.

[*Slow, motionless, barely articulate*

Tom

[*As she does not move he lifts his head. And even as
he looks at her, she does not move, nor look at him.*]
Claire — [*His hand out to her, a little afraid.*] You
went away from me then. You are away from me
now.

Claire

Yes, and I could go on. But I will come back. [*It
is hard to do. She brings much with her.*] That, too,
I will give you — my by-myself-ness. That's the uttermost I can give. I never thought — to try to give it.
But let us do it — the great sacrilege! Yes! [*Excited,
she rises; she has his hands, and brings him up beside
her.*] Let us take the mad chance! Perhaps it's the
only way to save — What's there. How do we know?
How can we know? Risk. Risk everything. From
all that flows into us, let it rise! All that we never
thought to use to make a moment — let it flow into
what could be! Bring all into life between us — or
send all down to death! Oh, do you know what I am
doing? Risk, risk everything. Why are you so afraid
to lose? What holds you from me? Test all. Let it
live or let it die. It is our chance — our chance to
bear — what's there. My dear one — I will love you
so. With all of me. I am not afraid now — of — all
of me. Be generous. Be unafraid. Life is for *life* —
though it cuts us from the farthest life. How can
I make you know that's true? All that we're open to —
[*Hesitates, shudders.*] But yes — I will, I will risk the
life that waits. Perhaps only he who gives his loneli-

ness — shall find. You never keep by holding. [*Gesture of giving.*] To the uttermost. And it is gone — or it is there. You do not know and — that makes the moment — [*Music has begun — a phonograph downstairs; they do not heed it.*] Just as I would cut my wrists — [*Holding them out.*] Yes, perhaps this lesser thing will tell it — would cut my wrists and let the blood flow out till all is gone if my last drop would make — would make —[*Looking at them fascinated.*] I want to see it doing that! Let me give my last chance for life to —

> [*He snatches her — they are on the brink of their moment; now that there are no words the phonograph from downstairs is louder. It is playing langorously the Barcarole; they become conscious of this — they do not want to be touched by the love song.*]

CLAIRE

Don't listen. That's nothing. This isn't that. [*Fearing.*] I tell you — it isn't that. Yes, I know — that's amorous — enclosing. I know — a little place. This isn't that. [*Her arms going around him — all the lure of " that " while she pleads against it as it comes up to them.*] We will come out — to radiance — in far places. [*Admitting, using.*] Oh, then let it be that! Go with it. Give up — the otherness. I will! And in the giving up — perhaps a door — we'd never find by searching. And if it's no more — than all have known, I only say — it's worth the allness! [*Her arms wrapped round him.*] My love — my love — let go your pride in loneliness and let me give you joy!

TOM

[*Drenched in her passion, but fighting.*] It's *you.* [*In anguish.*] You rare thing untouched — not — not into this — not back into this — by me — lover of your apartness.

> [*She steps back. She sees he cannot. She stands there, before what she wanted more than life, and almost had, and lost. A long moment. Then she runs down the stairs.*

CLAIRE

[*Her voice coming up.*] Harry! Choke that phonograph! If you want to be lewd — do it yourselves! You tawdry things — you cheap little lewd cowards — [*A door heard opening below.*] Harry! If you don't stop that music, I'll kill myself. [*Far down, steps on stairs.*

HARRY

Claire. what *is* this?

CLAIRE

Stop that phonograph or I'll —

HARRY

Why of course I'll stop it. What — what is there to get so excited about? Now — now just a minute, dear. It'll take a minute.

> [CLAIRE *comes back upstairs, dragging steps, face ghastly. The amorous song still comes up, and louder now, that doors are open. She and* TOM *do not look at one another. Then, on a langorous swell the music comes to a grating stop. They do not speak or move. Quick footsteps —* HARRY *comes up.*

HARRY

What in the world were you saying, Claire? Certainly you could have asked me more quietly to turn off the Victrola. Though what harm was it doing you

— way up here? [*A sharp little sound from* CLAIRE; *she checks it, her hand over her mouth.* HARRY *looks from her to* TOM.] Well I think you two would better have had your dinner. Won't you come down now and have some?

CLAIRE

[*Only now taking her hand from her mouth.*] Harry, tell him to come up here — that insanity man. I — want to ask him something.

HARRY

" Insanity man! " How absurd. He's a nerve specialist. There's a vast difference.

CLAIRE

Is there? Anyway, ask him to come up here. Want to — ask him something.

TOM

[*Speaking with difficulty.*] Wouldn't it be better for us to go down there?

CLAIRE

No. So nice up here! Everybody — up here!

HARRY

[*Worried.*] You'll — be yourself, will you, Claire? [*She checks a laugh, nods.*] I think he can help you.

CLAIRE

Want to ask him to — help me.

HARRY

[*As he is starting down.*] He's here as a guest tonight, you know, Claire.

CLAIRE

I suppose a guest can — help one.

Tom

[*When the silence rejects it.*] Claire, you must know, it's because it is so much, so —

Claire

Be still. There isn't anything to say.

Tom

[*Torn — tortured.*] If it only weren't *you!*

Claire

Yes, — so you said. If it weren't I. I suppose I wouldn't be so — interested!
> [*Hears them starting up below — keeps looking at the place where they will appear.*
> [Harry *is heard to call, " Coming,* Dick? " *and* Dick's *voice replies, " In a moment or two."* Adelaide *comes first.*

Adelaide

[*As her head appears.*] Well, these stairs should keep down weight. You missed an awfully good dinner, Claire. And kept Mr. Edgeworthy from a good dinner.

Claire

Yes. We missed our dinner.
> [*Her eyes do not leave the place where* Dr. Emmons *will come up.*]

Harry

[*As he and* Emmons *appear.*] Claire, this is —

Claire

Yes, I know who he is. I want to ask you —

ADELAIDE

Let the poor man get his breath before you ask him anything.

[*He nods, smiles, looks at* CLAIRE *with interest. Careful not to look too long at her, surveys the tower.*

EMMONS

Curious place.

ADELAIDE

Yes; it lacks form, doesn't it?

CLAIRE

What do you mean? How *dare* you?

[*It is impossible to ignore her agitation; she is backed against the curved wall, as far as possible from them.* HARRY *looks at her in alarm, then in resentment at* TOM *who takes a step nearer* CLAIRE.

HARRY

[*Trying to be light.*]   Don't take it so hard Claire.

CLAIRE

[*To Emmons.*]   It must be very interesting — helping people go insane.

ADELAIDE

Claire! How preposterous.

EMMONS

[*Easily.*]   I hope that's not precisely what we do.

ADELAIDE

[*With the smile of one who is going to " cover it."*] Trust Claire to put it in the unique and — amusing way.

CLAIRE

Amusing? You are amused? But it doesn't matter. [*To the doctor.*]   I think it is very kind of you — helping people go insane. I suppose they have all sorts of reasons for having to do it — reasons why they can't stay sane any longer. But tell me, how do they do it? It's not so easy to — get out. How do so many manage it?

EMMONS

I'd like immensely to have a talk with you about all this some day.

ADELAIDE

Certainly this is not the time, Claire.

CLAIRE

The time? When you — can't go any farther —isn't that —

ADELAIDE

[*Capably taking the whole thing into matter-of-factness.*] What I think is, Claire has worked too long with plants. There's something — not quite sound about making one thing into another thing. What we need is unity. [*From* CLAIRE *something like a moan.*] Yes dear, we do need it — [*To the doctor.*]   I can't say that I believe in making life *over* like this. I don't think the new species are worth it. At least I don't believe in it for Claire. If one is an intense, sensitive person —

CLAIRE

Isn't there any way to *stop* her? Always — always smothering it with the word for it?

EMMONS

[*Soothingly.*] But she can't smother it. Anything that's really there — she can't hurt with words.

CLAIRE

[*Looking at him with eyes too bright.*] Then you don't see it either. [*Angry.*] Yes, she can hurt it! Piling it up — always piling it up — between us and — What there. Clogging the way — always — [*To* EMMONS.] I want to cease to know! That's all I ask. Darken it. Darken it. If you came to help me, strike me blind!

EMMONS

You're really all tired out, aren't you? Oh, we've got to get you rested.

CLAIRE

They — deny it saying they have it; and he — [*half looks at* TOM — *quickly looks away*] others, deny it — afraid of losing it. We're in the *way*. Can't you see the dead stuff piled in the path?

[*Pointing.*

DICK

[*Voice coming up.*] Me too?

CLAIRE

[*Staring at the path, hearing his voice a moment after it has come.*] Yes, Dick — you too. Why not — you too. [*After he has come up.*] What is there any more than you are?

DICK

[*Embarrassed by the intensity, but laughing.*] A question not at all displeasing to me. Who can answer it?

CLAIRE

[*More and more excited.*] Yes! Who can answer it? [*Going to him, in terror.*] Let me go with you — and be with you — and know nothing else!

ADELAIDE

[*Gasping.*] Why — !

HARRY

Claire! This is going a little too —

CLAIRE

Far? But you have to go far to — [*Clinging to* DICK.] Only a place to hide your head — what else is there to hope for? I can't stay with them — piling it up! Always — piling it up! I can't get through to — he won't let me through to — what I don't know is there! [*As* DICK *would help her regain herself.*] Don't push me away! Don't — don't stand me up, I will go back — to the worst we ever were! Go back — and remember — what we've tried to forget!

ADELAIDE

It's time to stop this by force — if there's no other way.

[*The doctor shakes his head.*

CLAIRE

All I ask is to die in the gutter with everyone spitting on me. [*Changes to a curious weary smiling quiet.*] Still, why should they bother to do that?

HARRY

[*Brokenly.*] You're sick, Claire. There's no denying it.

[*Looks at* EMMONS, *who nods.*

ADELAIDE

Something to quiet her — to stop it.

CLAIRE

[*Throwing her arms around* DICK.] You, Dick. Not them. Not — any of them.

DICK

Claire, you are overwrought. You must —

HARRY

[*To* DICK, *as if only now realizing that phase of it.*]
I'll tell you one thing, you'll answer to me for this!
[*He starts for* DICK — *is restrained by*
EMMONS, *chiefly by his grave shake
of the head. With* HARRY'S *move to
them,* DICK *has shielded* CLAIRE.

CLAIRE

Yes — hold me. Keep me. You have mercy! You
will have mercy. Anything — everything — that will
let me be nothing!

[CURTAIN]

ACT THREE

In the greenhouse, the same as Act I. ANTHONY is bedding small plants where the Edge Vine grew. In the inner room the plant like caught motion glows as from a light within.

HATTIE, the Maid, rushes in from outside.

ANTHONY

[*Turning angrily.*] You are not what this place —

HATTIE

Anthony, come in the house. I'm afraid. Mr. Archer, I never saw him like this. He's talking to Mr. Demming — something about Mrs. Archer.

ANTHONY

[*Who in spite of himself is disturbed by her agitation.*] And if it is, it's no business of yours.

HATTIE

You don't know how he *is*. I went in the room and —

ANTHONY

Well, he won't hurt you, will he?

HATTIE

How do I know who he'll hurt — a person's whose — [*Seeing how to get him.*] Maybe he'll hurt Mrs. Archer.

ANTHONY

[*Startled, then smiles.*] No; he won't hurt Miss Claire.

HATTIE

What do you know about it? — out here in the plant house?

ANTHONY

And I don't want to know about it. This is a very important day for me. It's Breath of Life I'm thinking of today — not you and Mr. Archer.

HATTIE

Well suppose he does something to Mr. Demming?

ANTHONY

Mr. Demming will have to look out for himself, I am at work.

[*Resuming work.*

HATTIE

Don't you think I ought to tell Mrs. Archer that —

ANTHONY

You let her alone! This is no day for her to be bothered by you. At eleven o'clock — [*Looks at watch.*]
— she comes out here — to Breath of Life.

HATTIE

[*With greed for gossip.*] Did you see any of them when they came downstairs last night?

ANTHONY

I was attending to my own affairs.

HATTIE

They was all excited. Mr. Edgeworthy — he went away. He was gone all night, I guess. I saw him coming back just as the milkman woke me up. Now he's packing his things. *He* wanted to get to Mrs. Archer too — just a little while ago. But she won't open her door for none of them. I can't even get in to do her room.

ANTHONY

Then do some other room — and leave me alone in this room.

HATTIE

[*A little afraid of what she is asking.*] Is she *sick*, Anthony — or what? [*Vindicating herself, as he gives her a look.*] That doctor he stayed here late. But she'd locked herself in. I heard Mr. Archer —

ANTHONY

You heard too much!

[*He starts for the door, to make her leave, but* DICK *rushes in. Looks around wildly, goes to the trap door, finds it locked.*

ANTHONY

What are you doing here?

DICK

Trying not to be shot — if you must know. This is the only place I can think of — till he comes to his senses and I can get away. Open that, will you? Rather — ignominious — but better be absurd than be dead.

HATTIE

Has he got the revolver?

DICK

Gone for it. Thought I wouldn't sit there till he got back. [*To Anthony.*] Look here — don't you get the idea? Get me some place where he can't come.

ANTHONY

It is not what this place is for.

DICK

Any place is for saving a man's life.

HATTIE

Sure, Anthony. Mrs. Archer wouldn't want Mr. Demming shot.

DICK

That's right, Anthony. Miss Claire will be angry at you if you get me shot.
[*He makes for the door of the inner room.*

ANTHONY

You can't go in there. It's locked.
[HARRY *rushes in from outside.*

HARRY

I thought so!
[*He has the revolver.* HATTIE *screams.*

ANTHONY

Now Mr. Archer, if you'll just stop and think, you'll know Miss Claire wouldn't want Mr. Demming shot.

HARRY

You think that can stop me? You think you can stop me? [*Raising the revolver.*] A dog that —

ANTHONY

[*Keeping squarely between* HARRY *and* DICK.] Well, you can't shoot him in here. It is not good for the plants. [HARRY *is arrested by this reason.*] And especially not today. Why, Mr. Archer, Breath of Life may flower today. It's years Miss Claire's been working for this day.

HARRY

I never thought to see this day!

ANTHONY

No, did you? Oh, it will be a wonderful day. And how she has worked for it. She has an eye that sees what isn't right in what looks right. Many's the time

I've thought — Here the form is set — and then she'd
say " We'll try this one," and it had — what I hadn't
known was there. She's like that.

HARRY

I've always been pleased, Anthony, at the way
you've worked with Miss Claire. This is hardly the
time to stand there eulogizing her. And she's [*can
hardly say it*] things you don't know she is.

ANTHONY

[*Proudly.*] Oh, I know that! You think I could
work with her and not know she's more than I know
she is?

HARRY

Well if you love her you've got to let me shoot the
dirty dog that drags her down!

ANTHONY

Not in here. Not today. More than like you'd
break the glass. And Breath of Life's in there.

HARRY

Anthony, this is pretty clever of you — but —

ANTHONY

I'm not clever. But I know how easy it is to turn
life back. No, I'm not clever at all, [CLAIRE *has
appeared and is looking in from outside*] but I do know
— there are things you mustn't hurt. [*He sees her*].
Yes, here's Miss Claire.
        [SHE *comes in.   She is looking immaculate.*

CLAIRE

From the gutter I rise again, refreshed. One does,
you know. Nothing is fixed — not even the gutter.

[*Smilingly to* HARRY *and refusing to notice revolver or agitation.*] How did you like the way I entertained the nerve specialist?

HARRY

Claire! You can *joke* about it?

CLAIRE

[*Taking the revolver from the hand she has shocked to limpness.*] Whom are you trying to make hear?

HARRY

I'm trying to make the world hear that [*pointing*] there stands a dirty dog who —

CLAIRE

Listen, Harry. [*Turning to* HATTIE, *who is over by the tall plants at right, not wanting to be shot but not wanting to miss the conversation.*] You can do my room now, Hattie. [HATTIE *goes.*] If you're thinking of shooting Dick, you can't shoot him while he's backed up against that door.

ANTHONY

Just what I told them, Miss Claire. Just what I told them.

CLAIRE

And for that matter, it's quite dull of you to have any idea of shooting him.

HARRY

I may be dull — I know you think I am — but I'll show you that I've enough of the man in me to —

CLAIRE

To make yourself ridiculous? If I ran out and hid my head in the mud, would you think you had to shoot the mud?

DICK

[*Stung out of fear.*]   That's pretty cruel!

CLAIRE

Well, would you rather be shot?

HARRY

So you just said it to protect him!

CLAIRE

I change it to grass.   [*Nodding to* DICK.]   Grass.   If I hid my face in the grass, would you have to burn the grass?

HARRY

Oh, Claire, how *can* you?   When you know how I love you — and how I'm suffering?

CLAIRE

[*With interest.*]   Are you suffering?

HARRY

Haven't you *eyes?*

CLAIRE

I should think it would — do something to you.

HARRY

God!   Have you no heart?

[*The door opens.   Tom comes in.*

CLAIRE

[*Scarcely saying it.*]   Yes, I have a heart.

TOM

[*After a pause.*]   I came to say good-bye.

CLAIRE

God!   Have you no heart?   Can't you at least wait till Dick is shot?

TOM

Claire! [*Now sees the revolver in her hand that is turned from him. Going to her.*] Claire!

CLAIRE

And even you think this is so important? [*Carelessly raises the revolver, and with her left hand out flat, tells* TOM *not to touch her.*] Harry thinks it important he shoot Dick, and Dick thinks it important not to be shot, and you think I mustn't shoot anybody — even myself — and can't any of you see that none of that is as important as — where revolvers can't reach? [*Putting revolver where there is no Edge Vine.*] I shall never shoot myself. I'm too interested in destruction to cut it short by shooting. [*After looking from one to the other, laughs. Pointing.*] One — two — three. You-love-me. But why do you bring it out here?

ANTHONY

[*Who has resumed work.*] It is not what this place is for.

CLAIRE

No. This place is for the destruction that can get through.

ANTHONY

Miss Claire, it is eleven. At eleven we are to go in and see —

CLAIRE

Whether it has gone through. But how can we go — with Dick against that door?

ANTHONY

He'll have to move.

CLAIRE

And be shot?

HARRY

[*Irritably.*]   Oh, he'll not be shot.   Claire can spoil anything.

[DICK *steps away from the door;* CLAIRE *takes a step nearer it.*]

CLAIRE

[*Halting.*]   Have I spoiled everything?   I don't want to go in there.

ANTHONY

We're going in together, Miss Claire.   Don't you remember?   Oh — [*Looking resentfully at the others.*] — don't let any little thing spoil it for you — the work of all those days — the hope of so many days.

CLAIRE

Yes — that's 't.

ANTHONY

You're afraid you haven't done it?

CLAIRE

Yes, but — afraid I have.

HARRY

[*Cross, but kindly.*]   That's just nervousness, Claire. I've had the same feeling myself about making a record in flying.

CLAIRE

[*Curiously grateful.*]   You have, Harry?

HARRY

[*Glad enough to be back in a more usual world.*]   Sure. I've been afraid to know, and almost as afraid of having done it as of not having done it.

[CLAIRE *nods, steps nearer, then again pulls back.*

CLAIRE

I can't go in there. [*She almost looks at* TOM.] Not today

ANTHONY

But Miss Claire, there'll be things to see today we can't see tomorrow.

CLAIRE

You bring it in here!

ANTHONY

In — Out from its own place? [*She nods.*] And — where they are? [*Again she nods.*] [*Reluctantly he goes to the door.*] I will not look into the heart. No one must know before you know.

> [*In the inner room, his head a little turned away, he is seen very carefully to lift the plant which glows from within. As he brings it in, no one looks at it.* HARRY *takes a box of seedlings from a stand and puts them on the floor, that the newcomer may have a place.*

ANTHONY

Breath of Life is here, Miss Claire.

> [CLAIRE *half turns, then stops.*

CLAIRE

Look — and see — what you see.

ANTHONY

No one should see what you've not seen.

CLAIRE

I can't see — until I know.

> [ANTHONY *looks into the flower.*

ANTHONY

[*Agitated.*] Miss Claire!

CLAIRE

It has come through?

ANTHONY

It has gone on.

CLAIRE

Stronger?

ANTHONY

Stronger, surer.

CLAIRE

And more fragile?

ANTHONY

And more fragile.

CLAIRE

Look deep. No — turning back?

ANTHONY

[*After a searching look.*] The form is set.
                              [*He steps back from it.*

CLAIRE

Then it is — out. [*From where she stands she turns slowly to the plant.*] You weren't. You are.

ANTHONY

But come and see, Miss Claire.

CLAIRE

It's so much more than — I'd see.

HARRY

Well I'm going to see. [*Looking into it.*] I never saw anything like that before! There seems something alive — inside this outer shell.

DICK

[*He too looking in and he has an artist's manner of a hand up to make the light right.*] It's quite new in form. It — says something about form.

HARRY

[*Cordially to Claire, who stands apart.*] So you've really put it over. Well well,— congratulations. It's a good deal of a novelty, I should say, and I've no doubt you'll have a considerable success with it — people always like something new. I'm mighty glad — after all your work, and I hope it will — set you up.

CLAIRE

[*Low — and like a machine.*] Will you all — go away?
[*Anthony goes — into the other room.*

HARRY

Why — why, yes. But — oh, Claire! Can't you take some pleasure in your work? [*As she stands there very still.*] Emmons says you need a good long rest — and I think he's right.

TOM

Can't this help you, Claire? Let this be release. This — breath of the uncaptured.

CLAIRE

[*And though speaking, she remains just as still.*]
Breath of the uncaptured?
You are a novelty.
Out?
You have been brought in.
A thousand years from now, when you are but a form too long repeated,
Perhaps the madness that gave you birth will burst again,

And from the prison that is you will leap pent queer-
nesses
To make a form that hasn't been —
To make a prison new.
And this we call creation.

> [*Very low, her head not coming up.*

Go away!

> [TOM *goes;* HARRY *hesitates, looking in
> anxiety at Claire. He starts to go,
> stops, looks at Dick, from him to
> Claire. But goes. A moment later,
> Dick moves near Claire; stands uncer-
> tainly, then puts a hand upon her.
> She starts, only then knowing he is
> there.*

CLAIRE

[*A slight shrinking away, but not really reached.*]
Um, um. . . .

> [*He goes. Claire steps nearer her creation.
> She looks into what hasn't been.
> With her breath, and by a gentle
> moving of her hands, she fans it to
> fuller openness. As she does this*
> TOM *returns and from outside is
> looking in at her. Softly he opens the
> door and comes in. She does not
> know that he is there. In the way
> she looks at the flower he looks at her.*

TOM

Claire — [*She lifts her head.*] As you stood there,
looking into the womb you breathed to life, you were
beautiful to me beyond any other beauty. You were
life and its reach and its anguish. I can't go away from
you. I will never go away from you. It shall all be —
as you wish. I can go with you where I could not go
alone. If this is delusion, I want that delusion. It's

more than any reality I could attain. [*As she does not move.*] Speak to me, Claire. You — are glad?

CLAIRE

[*From far.*] Speak to you? [*Pause.*] Do I know who you are?

TOM

I think you do.

CLAIRE

Oh, yes. I love you. That's who you are. [*Waits again.*] But why are you something — very far away?

TOM

Come nearer.

CLAIRE

Nearer? [*Feeling it with her voice.*] Nearer. But I think I am going — the other way.

TOM

No, Claire — come to me. Did you understand, dear. I am not going away.

CLAIRE

You're not going away?

TOM

Not without you, Claire. And you and I will be together. Is that — what you wanted?

CLAIRE

Wanted? [*As if wanting is something that harks far back. But the word calls to her passion.*] Wanted! [*A sob, hands out, she goes to him. But before his arms can take her, she steps back.*] Are you trying to pull me down into what I wanted? Are you here to make me stop?

TOM

How can you ask that? I love you because it is not in you to stop.

CLAIRE

And loving me for that — would stop me? Oh, help me see it! It is so important that I see it.

TOM

It is important. It is our lives.

CLAIRE

And more than that. I cannot see it because it is so much more than that.

TOM

Don't try to see all that it is. From peace you'll see a little more.

CLAIRE

Peace? [*Troubled as we are when looking at what we cannot see clearly.*] What is peace? Peace is what the struggle knows in moments very far apart. Peace — that is not a place to rest. Are you resting? What are you? You who'd take me from what I am to something else?

TOM!

I thought you knew, Claire.

CLAIRE

I know — what you pass for. But are you beauty? Beauty is that only living pattern — the trying to take pattern. Are you trying?

TOM

Within myself, Claire. I never thought you doubted that.

CLAIRE

Beauty is — [*She turns to Breath of Life, as if to learn it there, but turns away with a sob.*] If I cannot go to you now — I will always be alone.

[TOM *takes her in his arms. She is shaken, then comes to rest.*]

TOM

Yes — rest. And then — come into joy. You have so much life for joy.

CLAIRE

[*Raising her head, called by promised gladness.*] We'll run around together. [*Lovingly he nods.*] Up hills. All night on hills.

TOM

[*Tenderly.*] All night on hills.

CLAIRE

We'll go on the sea in a little boat.

TOM

On the sea in a little boat.

CLAIRE

But — there are other boats on other seas. [*Drawing back from him, troubled.*] There are other boats on other seas.

TOM

[*Drawing her back to him.*] My dearest — not now, not now.

CLAIRE

[*Her arms going round him.*] Oh, I would love those hours with you. I want them. I want you! [*They kiss — but deep in her is sobbing.*] Reminiscence. [*Her hand feeling his arm as we touch what we would remember.*] Reminiscence. [*With one of her swift changes steps back from him.*] How dare you pass for what you're not? We, are tired, and so we think it's you. Stop with you. Don't get through — to what you're in the way of. Beauty is not something you say about beauty.

TOM

I say little about beauty, Claire.

CLAIRE

Your life says it. By standing far off you pass for it. Smother it with a life that passes for it. But beauty — [*Getting it from the flower.*] Beauty is the humility breathed from the shame of succeeding.

TOM

But it may all be within one's self, dear.

CLAIRE

[*Drawn by this, but held, and desperate because she is held.*] When I have wanted you with all my wanting — why must I distrust you now? When I love you — with all of me, why do I know that only you are worth my hate?

TOM

It's the fear of easy satisfactions. I love you for it.

CLAIRE

[*Over the flower.*] Breath of Life — you here? Are you lonely — Breath of Life?

TOM

Claire — hear me! Don't go where we can't go. As there you made a shell for life within, make for yourself a life in which to live. It must be so.

CLAIRE

As you made for yourself a shell called beauty?

TOM

What is there for you, if you'll have no touch with what we have?

CLAIRE

What is there? There are the dreams we haven't dreamed. There is that long and flowing pattern — [*She follows that but suddenly and as if blindly, goes to him.*] I am tired. I am lonely. I'm afraid. [*He holds her, soothing. But she steps back from him.*] and because we are tired — lonely — and afraid, we stop with you. Don't get through — to what you're in the way of.

TOM

Then you don't love me?

CLAIRE

I'm fighting for my chance. I don't know — which chance.

> [*Is drawn to the other chance, to Breath of Life. Looks into it as if to look through to the uncaptured. And through this life just caught comes the truth she chants.*]

I've wallowed at a coarse man's feet,
I'm sprayed with dreams we've not yet come to.
I've gone so low that words can't get there,
I've never pulled the mantle of my fears around me
And called it loneliness — And called it God.
Only with life that waits have I kept faith.
> [*With effort raising her eyes to the man.*
And only you have ever threatened me.

TOM

[*Coming to her, and with strength now.*] And I will threaten you. I'm here to hold you from where I know you cannot go. You're trying what we can't do.

CLAIRE

What else is there worth trying?

TOM

I love you, and I will keep you — from fartherness
— from harm. You are mine, and you will stay with
me! [*Roughly*.] You hear me? You will stay with me!

CLAIRE

[*Her head on his breast, in ecstacy of rest. Drowsily*.]
You can keep me?

TOM

Darling! I can keep you. I will keep you — safe.

CLAIRE

[*Troubled by the word, but barely able to raise her head*.]
Safe?

TOM

[*Bringing her to rest again*.] Trust me, Claire.

CLAIRE

[*Not lifting her head, but turning it so she sees Breath
of Life*.] Now can I trust — what is? [*Suddenly
pushing him roughly away*.] No! I will beat my life
to pieces in the struggle to —

TOM

To *what*, Claire?

CLAIRE

Not to stop it by seeming to have it. [*With fury*.]
I will keep my life low — low — that I may never stop
myself — or any one — with the thought it's what *I*
have. I'd rather be the steam rising from the manure
than be a thing called beautiful! [*With sight too clear*.]
Now I know who you are. It is you puts out the breath
of life. Image of beauty — *You fill the place — should
be a gate*. [*In agony*.] Oh, that it is *you* — fill the

place — should be a gate! My darling! That it should be you who — [*Her hands moving on him.*] Let me tell you something. Never was loving strong as my loving of you! Do you know that? Oh, know that! Know it now! [*Her arms go around his neck.*] Hours with you — I'd give my life to have! That it should be you — [*He would loosen her hands, for he cannot breathe. But when she knows she is choking him, that knowledge is fire burning its way into the last passion.*] It *is* you. It is you.

TOM

[*Words coming from a throat not free.*]   Claire! What are you doing?

> [*Then she knows what she is doing.*

CLAIRE

[*To his resistance.*]   No! You are *too much!*   You are *not enough.*   [*Still wanting not to hurt her, he is slow in getting free. He keeps stepping backward trying, in growing earnest, to loosen her hands. But he does not loosen them before she has found the place in his throat that cuts off breath.   As he gasps.*]   Breath of Life — my gift — to you!

> [*She has pushed him against one of the plants at right as he sways, strength she never had before pushes him over backward, just as they have struggled from sight. Violent crash of glass is heard.*

TOM

[*Faint smothered voice.*]   No.   I'm — hurt.

CLAIRE

[*In the frenzy and agony of killing.*]   Oh gift! Oh gift! [*There is no sound.   CLAIRE rises — steps back — is seen now; is looking down.*]   Gift.

> [*Like one who does not know where she is, she moves into the room — looks around. Takes a step toward Breath of Life, turns and goes quickly to the door. Stops, as if stopped. Sees the revolver where the Edge Vine was. Slowly goes to it. Holds it as if she cannot think what it is for. Then raises it high and fires above through the place in the glass left open for ventilation.*
>
> [ANTHONY *comes from the inner room. His eyes go from her to the body beyond.* HARRY *rushes in from outside.*

HARRY

Who fired that?

CLAIRE

I did.   Lonely.

> [*Seeing* ANTHONY's *look,* HARRY's *eyes follow it.*

HARRY

Oh! What? What?   [DICK *comes running in.*] Who? Claire!

> [DICK *sees — goes to* TOM.

CLAIRE

Yes.   I did it.   MY — Gift.

HARRY

Is he —?   He isn't —?   He *isn't* —?

> [*Tries to go in there. Cannot — there is the sound of broken glass, of a position being changed — then* DICK *reappears.*

DICK

[*His voice in jerks.*]   It's — it's no use, but I'll go for a doctor.

HARRY

No — no. Oh, I suppose —[*Falling down beside* CLAIRE — *his face against her.*] My darling! How can I save you now?

CLAIRE

[*Speaking each word very carefully.*] Saved — myself.

ANTHONY

I did it. Don't you see? I didn't want so many around. Not — what this place is for.

HARRY

[*Snatching at this but lets it go.*] She wouldn't let — [*Looking up at* CLAIRE — *then quickly hiding his face.*] And — don't you see?

CLAIRE

Out. [*A little like a child's pleased surprise.*] Out [DICK *stands there, as if unable to get to the door — his face distorted, biting his hand.*

ANTHONY

Miss Claire! You can do anything — won't you *try?*

CLAIRE

Reminiscence?
[*Speaking the word as if she has left even that, but smiles a little.*
[ANTHONY *takes Reminiscence, the flower she was breeding for fragrance for Breath of Life — holds it out to her. But she has taken a step forward, past them all.*

CLAIRE

Out.

[*As if feeling her way.*

Nearer,

                       [Her voice now feeling the way to it.

Nearer —

                                 [Voice almost upon it.

— my *God.*

                       [Falling upon it with surprise.

To Thee,

                                      [Breathing it.

Nearer — to Thee,
   E'en though it be —

        [A slight turn of the head toward the dead
         man she loves — a mechanical turn
         just as far the other way.
              a cross

That

                              [Her head going down.

raises me;

             [Her head slowly coming up—singing it.
Still all my song shall be
Nearer my —

       [Slowly the curtain begins to shut her out.
       The last word heard is the final
       Nearer — a faint breath from far.

                          [CURTAIN]